MONTROSE

THE POSTCARD COLLECTION

Tom Valentine

AMBERLEY

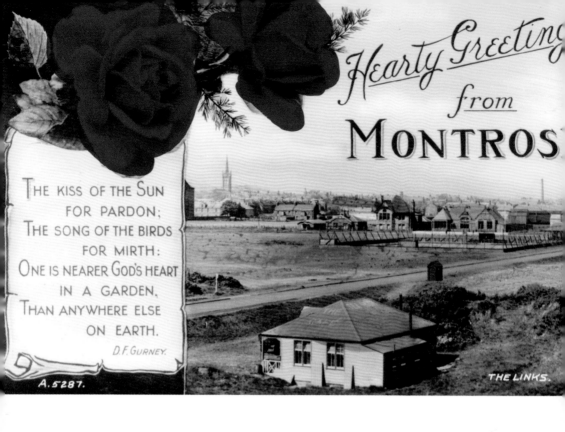

Front cover: A busy beach scene looking south towards Scurdyness Lighthouse, *c.* 1920.

First published 2014

Amberley Publishing
The Hill, Stroud, Gloucestershire, GL5 4EP
www.amberley-books.com

Copyright © Tom Valentine, 2014

The right of Tom Valentine to be identified as the
Author of this work has been asserted in accordance with
the Copyrights, Designs and Patents Act 1988.

ISBN 978 1 4456 3612 2 (print)
ISBN 978 1 4456 3640 5 (ebook)

British Library Cataloguing in Publication Data.
A catalogue record for this book is available from the
British Library.

Typesetting by Amberley Publishing.
Printed in Great Britain.

CONTENTS

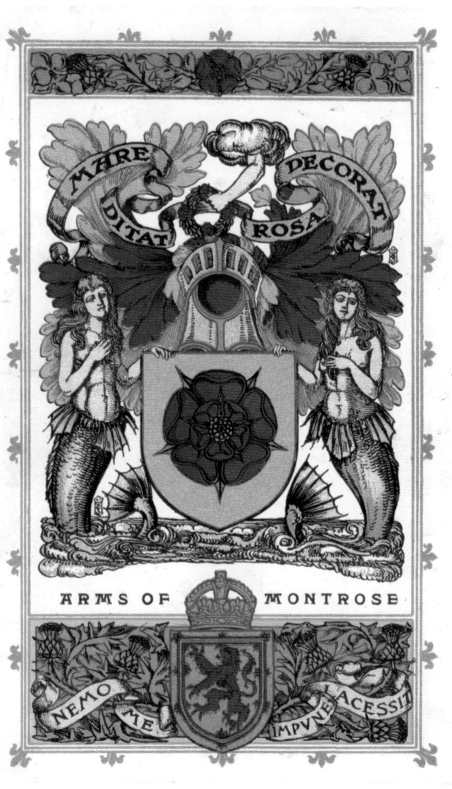

MARE DITAT ROSA DECORAT

ARMS OF MONTROSE

NEMO ME IMPVNE LACESSIT

INTRODUCTION

Midway between Aberdeen and Dundee, on the windswept east coast of Scotland, lies the town of Montrose. The ancient name of Montrose was *Celurca*. In British history, the name is given as *Manterose* (the mouth of the stream), while in Gaelic it appears as *Mon-ross* (the promontory hill). It has frequently been said the Montrose is a place of high antiquity, and witnessed many stirring and historic events. Montrose is positioned between the estuaries of the rivers North Esk and the South Esk, and on the west is a tidal basin more than 2 miles wide, and on the east is the North Sea.

The salmon fishers trailed their nets in Montrose Basin, and the mussel-gatherers collected their bait and have done this from time immemorial. From autumn until spring, the plaintive cry of wild geese can be heard echoing in the night sky as they wing their way over the town. A tenth of all the pink-footed geese in the world come here each year from their Arctic breeding grounds to winter around the basin. The High Street, which once had a row of houses down the centre, is as broad as two ordinary streets, and there are still gable-ended houses close to 300 years old that give it a Flemish air. Few streets in Scotland or England equal it in character. In the High Street, there are many closes with secluded gardens that were used by the smugglers in days gone by. It was down those closes that wealthy citizens built their mansions, and they serve as a reminder that this is a town with a history that goes back over 800 years.

At the south end of the High Street is a landmark that can be seen for miles around. This is the old church steeple, which had its foundation laid in 1832. To the west of the High Street you will find the main Aberdeen to Dundee railway line, as well as the West End Park, bounded on one side by large walls that were intended to keep out invaders. At one time, the water from the basin came up near to those walls, long before the West End Park existed. To the east of the High Street can be found the recently refurbished Mid Links, with its lovely parks, gardens and monuments. Also found here are Montrose's beautiful Grecian-style museum, bowling greens, and tennis courts. Further east can be found Montrose football ground and cricket pitch, then the grassy links and lovely, sandy beach. At the north end of the grassy links is where you will find Montrose's two golf courses. At the south end of the town is where the busy harbour can be found; this has steadily grown over the years due to the sea oil base that was built in the 1970s, after the South Esk Estuary was dredged and its land reclaimed.

Montrose has welcomed many famous people with notable connections. These include, to name just a few, James Graham, the 1st Marquess of Montrose, Joseph Hume, a Scottish doctor and politician, Violet Jacob, a Scottish writer, and Andrew Melville, a radical Presbyterian.

To the north of Montrose you will find the village of Hillside, where the recently closed Sunnyside Hospital was situated. A further few miles north can be found the village of Craigo, which once had a thriving jute mill. To the south of Montrose can be found the old fishing village of Ferryden, where there were once 160 fishing boats and 350 fishermen and an equal number of fisherwomen. Beyond Ferryden can be found the old fishing village of Usan, where the main row of houses that the locals once stayed in are now empty and in a ruined state. This village was first recorded in 1548, but possibly existed earlier.

Born in Montrose, I have always taken an interest in the history of the town, which has a fascinating story to tell. A good way to show this is through postcard images, which show how life was in times gone by.

My interest in collecting old postcards came by accident in the early 1970s, while on holiday in London. There I visited a philatelic fair in the Café Royal, Piccadilly. I noticed that several of the stallholders were selling old postcards, and I started looking through them with great interest. Nowadays, there are a great deal of postcard fairs across the country and dealers usually have their postcards in county order so it is easy to find postcards from a particular area. Back then in London, however, this was not so, and all the Scottish cards were mixed. It took a while to look through boxes to find a certain place but, at the end of the day, I found several Montrose and district postcards, and a new hobby began.

The postcards included in this book date from the 1890s to the 1940s, and the reader will see that some views have changed a lot while others have changed only a little. Montrose's motto translates as 'the sea enriches and the rose adorns', and this collection of old postcards hopes to show the reader how true this is.

BIBLIOGRAPHY

Adams, David G., *Usan or Fishtown of Ullishaven* (Chanory P. 1989)

Brown Gibson Jnr., James, *Angus Scenes Before World War I* (2001)

Hay, Kenneth M.; Aitken, John, *In the Wake of the Lochside* (John Aitken,1983)

Johns, Trevor W., *The Mid Links, Montrose Since Provost Scott 1883–1988* (Montrose Review Press, 1988)

Morrison, Dorothy; Mouat, Alex I., *Montrose Old Church: A History* (Montrose Old Church Bicentennary Committee)

West, Joe, *A Short History of Rossie Island and the Connecting Bridges* (Privately Published)

West, Joe, *A Personal History of Ferryden* (J. West, 1980s)

Society of Aero Historians, USA, *Cross & Cockade Journal* (Spring 1975)

Various Montrose Year Books and Directories

SECTION 1
STREETS

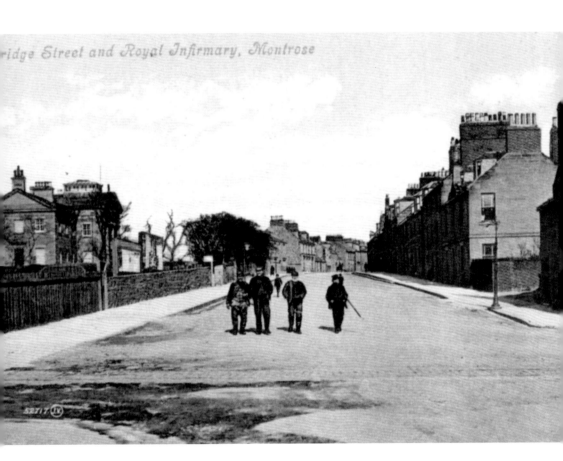

ridge Street and Royal Infirmary, Montrose

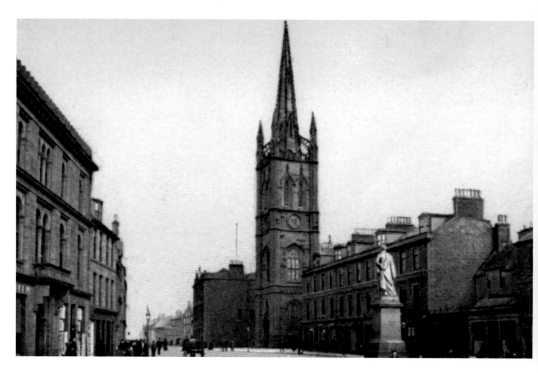

Peel Place

Two views of Peel Place looking north, which carries on to the start of the High Street. The view above shows the church steeple and the Robert Peel statue. The view below shows the west side of the street. On the extreme left can be seen the small building that housed Duthie's Union Inn. This was demolished to make way for the Montrose Library.

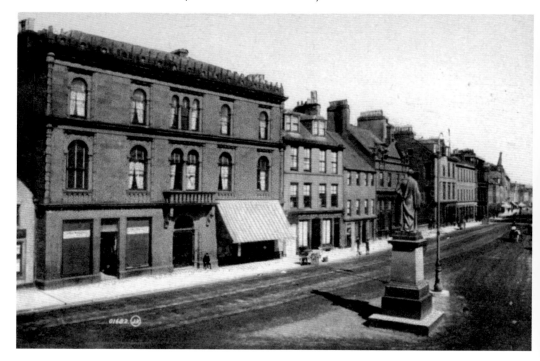

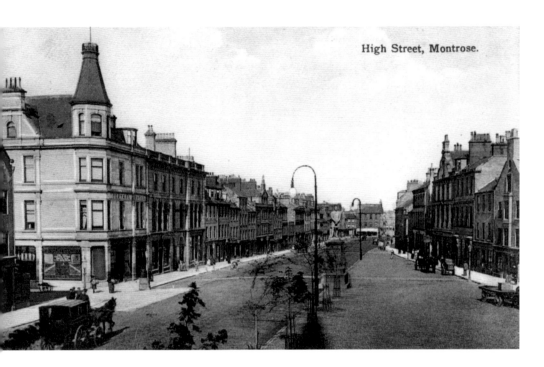

High Street, Montrose.

High Street

The High Street takes you from Peel Place to Murray Street. The postcard above is a view looking north, showing the statue of Joseph Hume, the Scottish doctor, who was born in Montrose. The postcard below shows the High Street, looking south, and the church steeple is again in full view. Aeroplanes were added in by the postcard publishers around 1913, when the Royal Flying Corps arrived in the area.

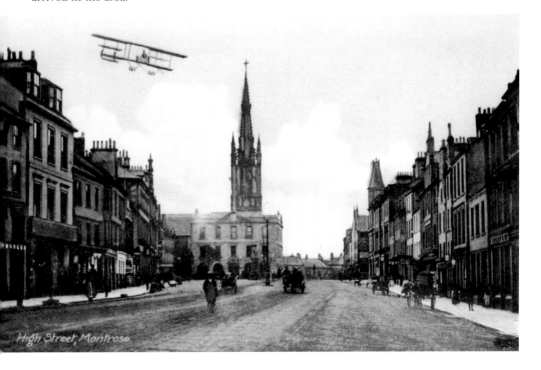

High Street, Montrose

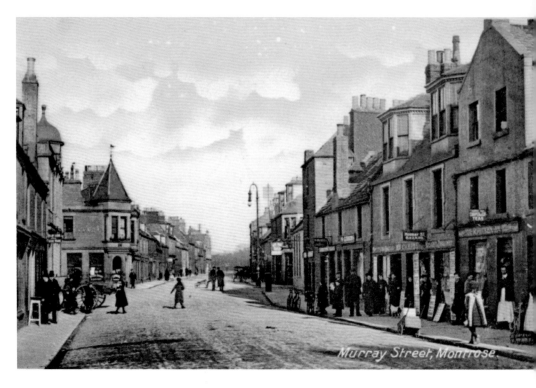

Murray Street

Murray Street was a street full of bazaars and cafés. The above postcard is looking north and takes you to North Esk Road. The postcard below is looking south towards the High Street, and dates from around 1918. The entrance to the High Street was called 'The Port'.

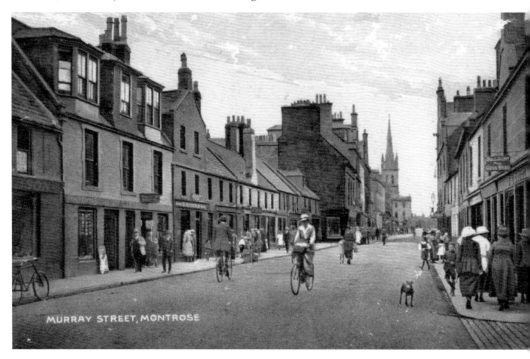

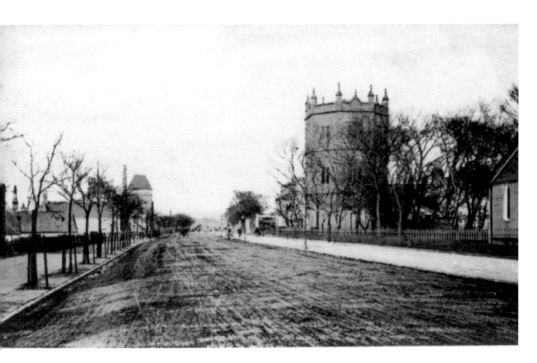

North Esk Road

The above postcard of North Esk Road is a view looking north, and takes you on to the Victoria Bridge and then on to either the Hillside or Charlton roads. The old water tower and the Lochside church can be seen on the right. The now demolished Lochside Distillery can be seen on the far left. The postcard below is a view looking south, with the Lochside Distillery buildings can be seen on the near right.

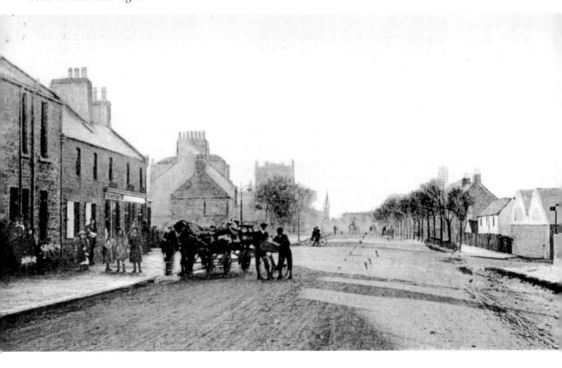

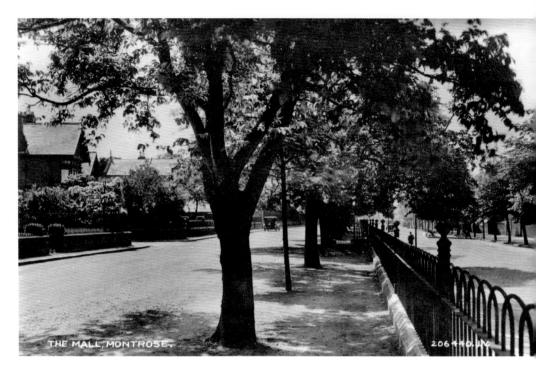

The Mall

The Mall is one of the finest picturesque promenades in the town. The top postcard is looking south, while the bottom view is looking north. The iron railings next to North Esk Road were left during the Second World War, probably due to the dangers of a sheer drop on to the pavement. The ones on the walls of the private housing were all removed.

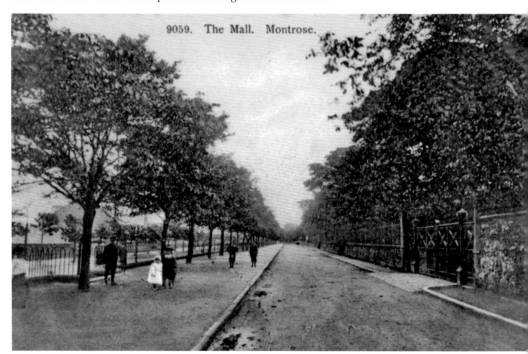

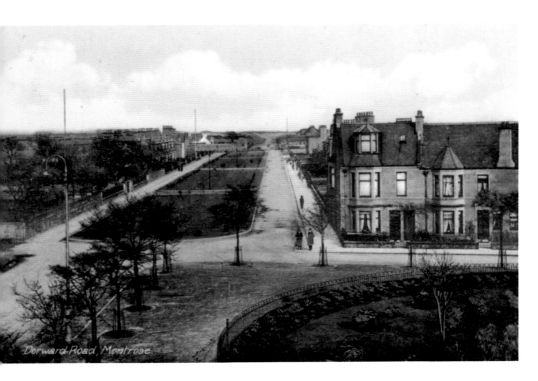

Dorward Road, Montrose.

Dorward Road

The postcard above shows Dorward Road looking east towards the start of the Traill Drive. This view was taken from the top of the North Links School. The gate and front grounds of Dorward House of Refuge can be seen at the near left. Dorward Street (Road) is shown on the postcard below, looking west towards the now demolished North Links School.

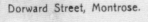

Dorward Street, Montrose.

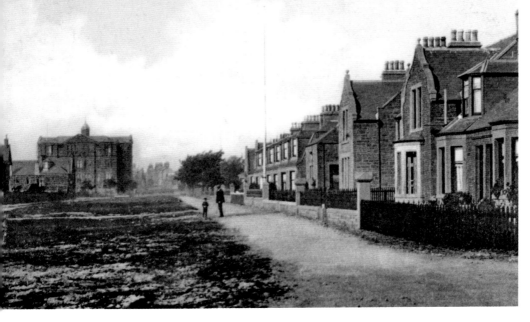

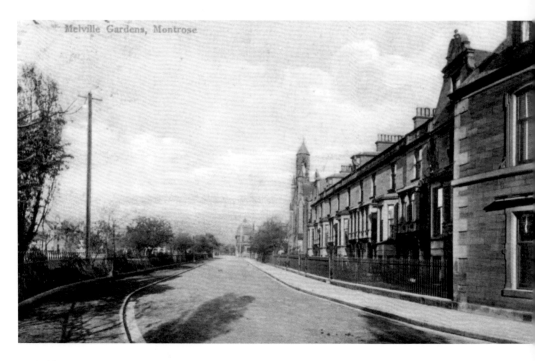

Melville Gardens and Ferry Street

The postcard above shows Melville Gardens looking north towards the Montrose Academy at the far end. The Melville church can be seen on the right, which is now the Montrose Town Hall. The lower postcard shows Ferry Street looking up towards George Street. The shops on the right have all gone and are now private residences. This street took you down to the docks, which have been filled in and have storage sheds built on top.

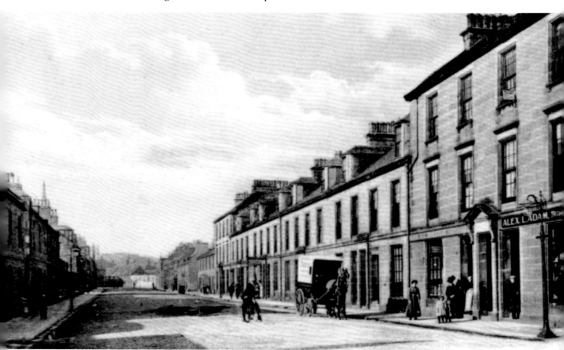

SECTION 2
BOATS & FISHING

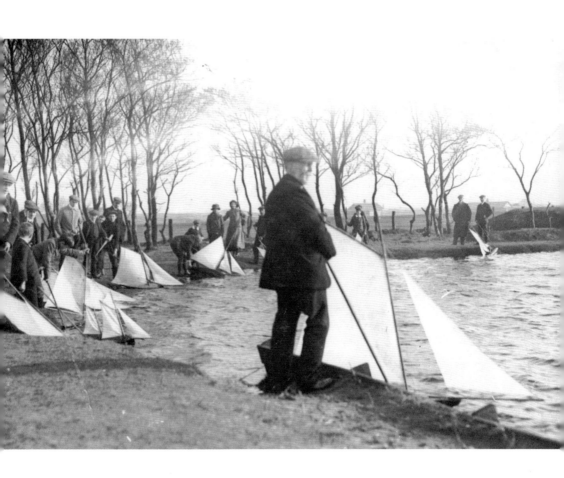

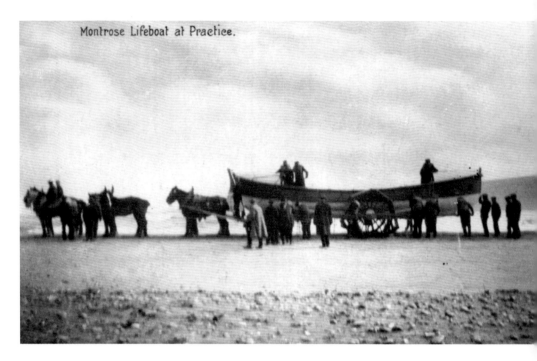
Montrose Lifeboat at Practice.

Montrose Lifeboats

The first Montrose Lifeboat Station was established in 1800, and the first lifeboat was built by Henry Greathead of South Shields. The above view of around 1900 shows the crew having lifeboat practice on the beach. The postcard below shows HRH The Duchess of York at Montrose to christen the new lifeboat *John Russell* on 18 September 1926. This generated tremendous excitement and interest in the town.

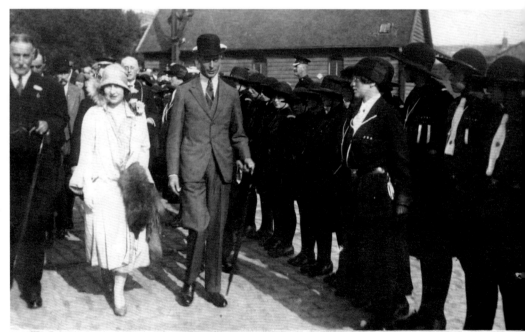
H. R. H. Duchess of York Christens Life Boat Montrose. 18 Sep 1926.

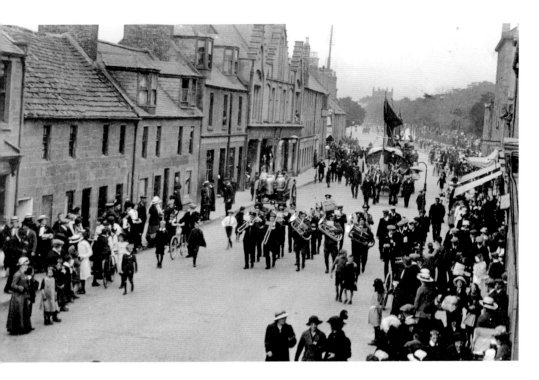

Lifeboat Parades

Lifeboat parades were very popular in the early part of the twentieth century. Here are two views of a parade heading south through Murray Street towards the High Street. The lifeboat was put on wheels and pulled by Clydesdale horses. Other parties joined in this parade, including scouts and young sailors, who were all led by the local town band. At the tail end is a wagon with model boats.

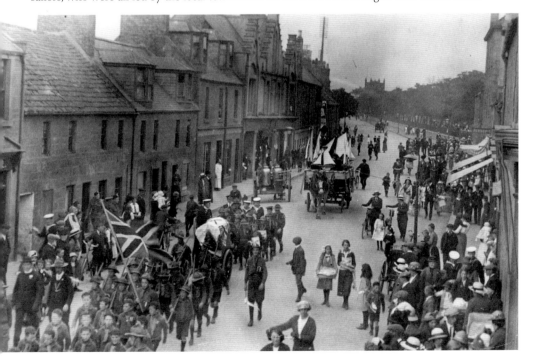

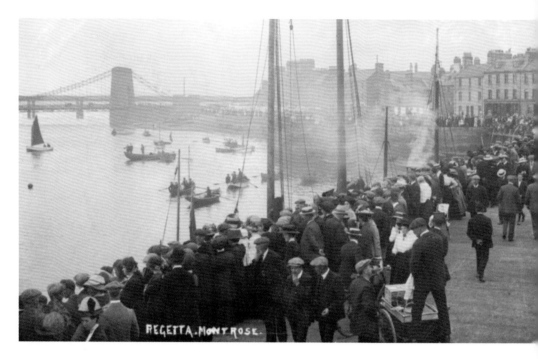

REGATTA . MONTROSE .

Regatta

These two postcards of around 1905 show a boating regatta on the estuary of the River South Esk. In the above postcard, crowds can be seen along the jetty from Wharf Street to the Suspension Bridge. The postcard below shows one of the boats with its four rowers and lead man passing the east end of Ferryden. These two postcards were published by one of Montrose's private photographers, J. G. Brown, who had his studio at No. 14 High Street.

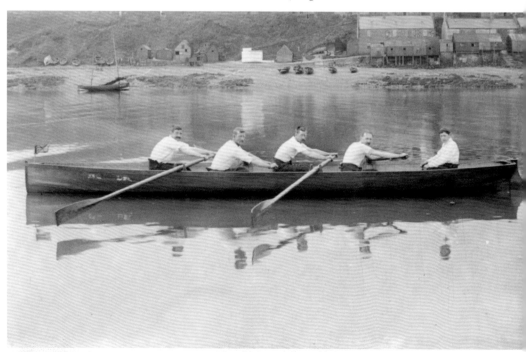

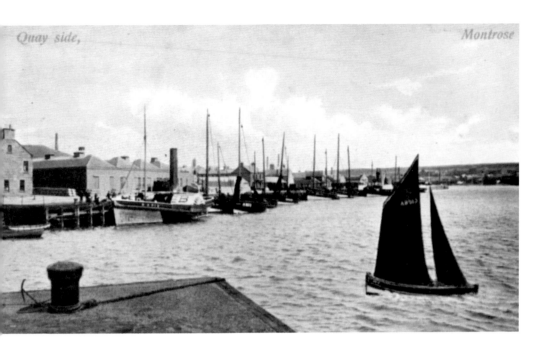

Quayside

The quayside was always very busy with fishing boats and paddle steamers. Here are two postcards showing views near the Wharf Street end of the quayside. During the Second World War, the buildings on the left, which were occupied by Chivers, were badly damaged by German war planes. The Beer Boat ('The Beerie') was a regular visitor at Montrose and steamed to the Tyne, carrying beer in hogsheads, barrels, halfies, quarters and firkins – her cargo having been brewed in James Deuchar's Lochside Brewery at the north end of town.

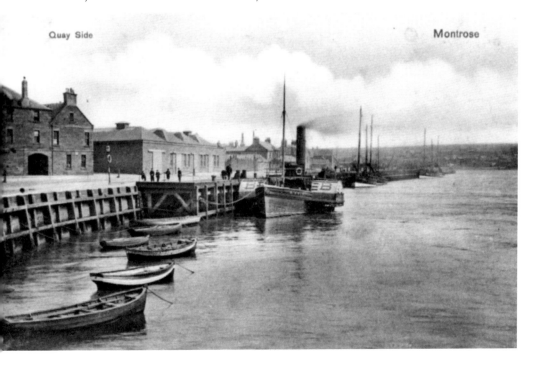

Quay Side   Montrose

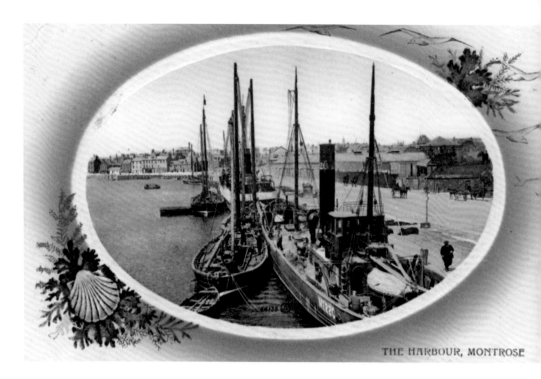

THE HARBOUR, MONTROSE

The Harbour and Docks

The postcard above shows a view of fishing boats tied up at the Montrose jetty, looking west towards Wharf Street. The postcard below is a view of the Montrose Docks, showing the dock buildings in the background. At the beginning of July 1981, the project of filling in this dock began by using of large diameter steel pipes to enable sand and stones, dredged from the bed of the River South Esk, to be pumped into the dock.

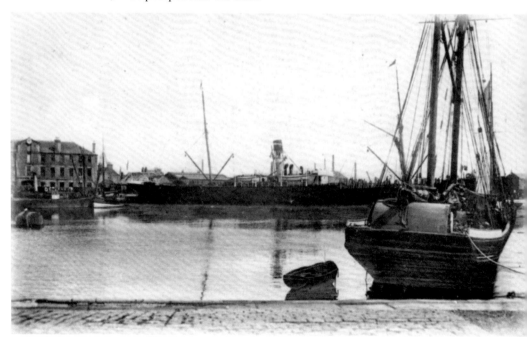

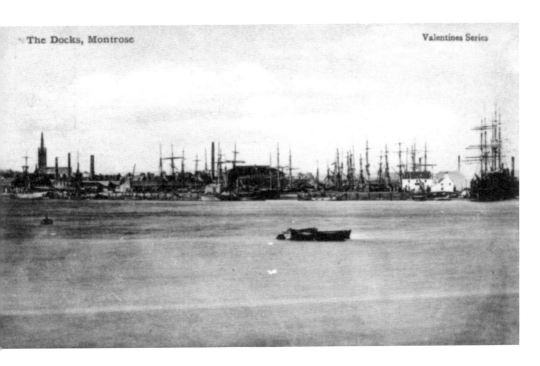

The Docks

The postcard above shows an early view of a very busy Montrose harbour around 1898. The dock on the right looks about full and boats are nearly nose to tail in the jetty area. The postcard below shows a Ferryden herring boat arriving back from the sea with its catch. After the boat arrived, the herring would need to be cleaned and packed into barrels, with salt (brine) being placed between each layer. This work could last all day and through the night if necessary.

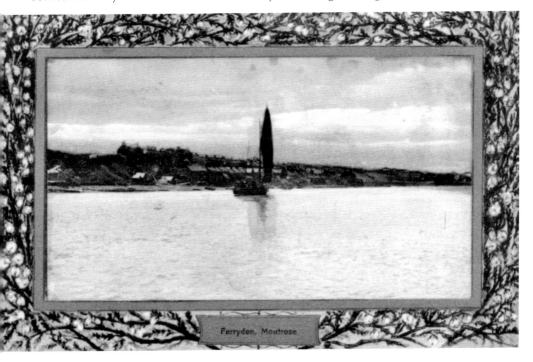

Ferryden, Montrose

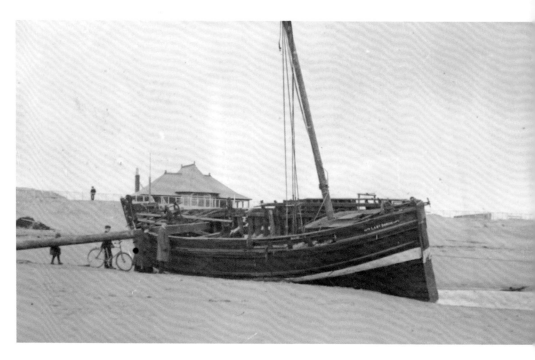

Lady Dorcas and *Ban Hong Liong*

The postcard above, dated 1913, shows the wreck of the *Lady Dorcas* fishing boat, which had run aground on Montrose Beach. This looks like it was before the Traill Pavilion was built, as only the Beach Pavilion can be seen in the background. Even to this day, parts of boats from years gone by are regularly found on the beach. The postcard below shows the launching of the *Ban Hong Liong* at Rossie Island boatyard. It is captioned on the reverse that this was the largest boat to date (1906) ever launched at Montrose.

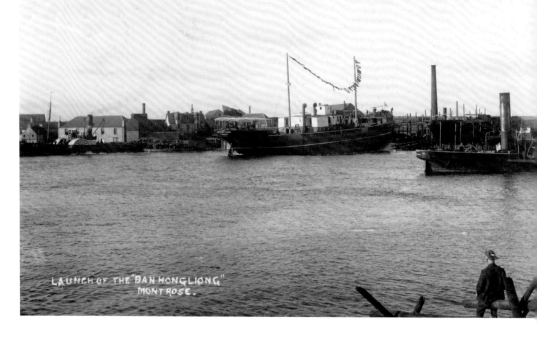

LAUNCH OF THE "BAN HONGLIONG"
MONTROSE.

SECTION 3
EVENTS

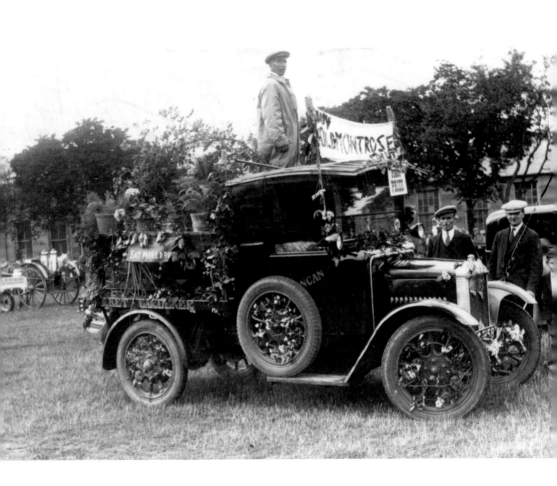

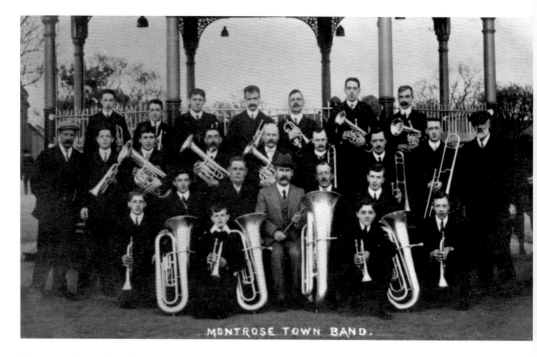

Montrose Town Band

These two postcards show the Montrose town band. The first is a *c.* 1915 view of them in front of the now demolished bandstand in the Mid Links, and the other is in front of the Traill Pavilion at the beach front in 1935. The band has now been in existence for 120 years and has its own hall in the Queen's Close off the southern end of the High Street. They have been stationed there since the mid-1950s and previous to this they practiced in a building in Orange Lane.

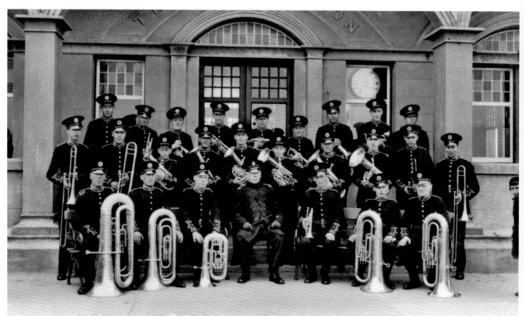

MONTROSE TOWN BAND 1935

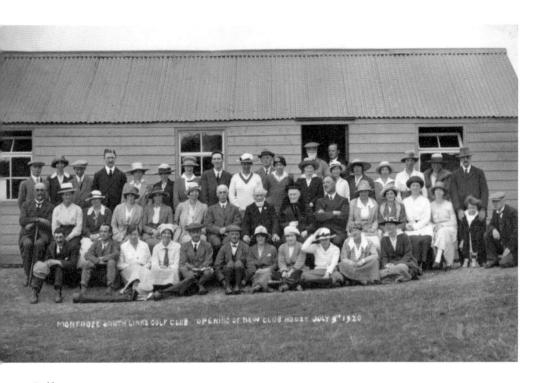

Golf

Golf has been played at Montrose for hundreds of years and has the fifth oldest golf course in the world. The postcard above shows the opening of the new clubhouse for the South Links Golf Club on 3 July 1920. Below is a golf bazaar being held in the drill hall in Mill Street around 1908 to raise funds for their club.

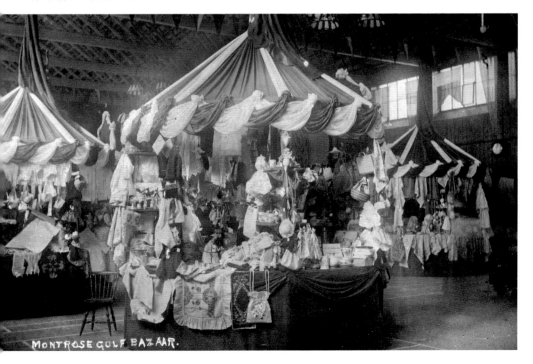

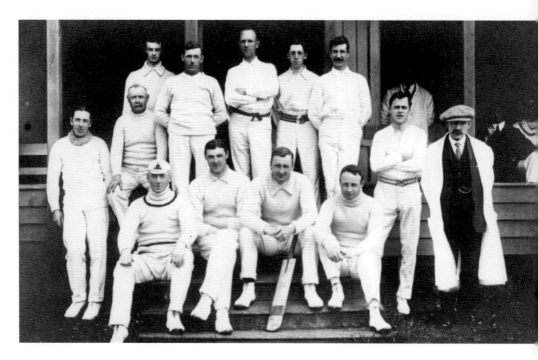

Montrose Cricket Club and Nurses at Hudson Square

Montrose Cricket Club was established in 1888, and the first match recorded was in 1849. The above postcard shows the Montrose team around 1915 in front of their clubhouse, probably taken at an event or before a special game. This was taken by private Montrose photographer J. G. Brown. The postcard below was photographed by Dunn, a photographer from Brechin, and is of a group of nurses at Hudson Square in Baltic Street. The event is unknown.

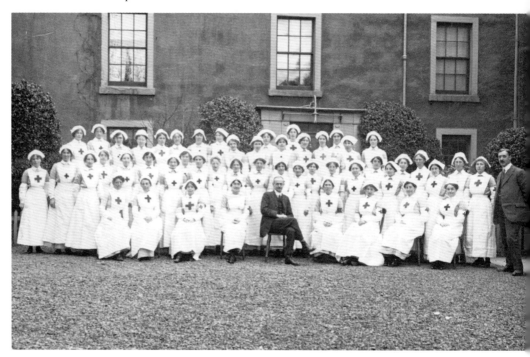

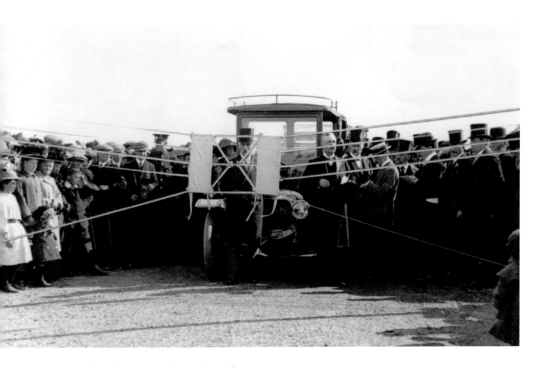

Opening of Traill Drive and Traill Pavilion

John Traill of Melbourne and his brother David Traill of West Bromwich, who were born in the town, donated two gifts of money to Montrose. The money was partly used to form the Traill Drive and to build the Traill Pavilion. The postcard above shows the opening of the Traill Drive in 1912, and the postcard below shows the opening of the Traill Pavilion in 1913. The Traill Drive starts at the bottom of Dorward Road and takes you past the golf courses, round the beachfront, and the Traill Pavillion, and finishes at Marine Avenue.

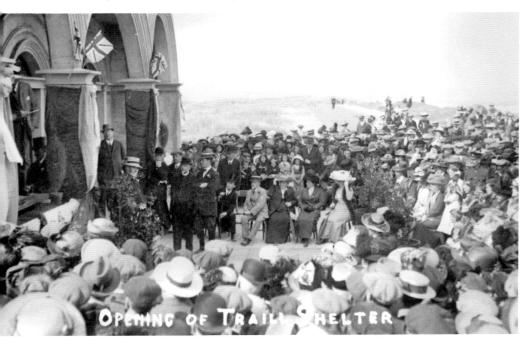

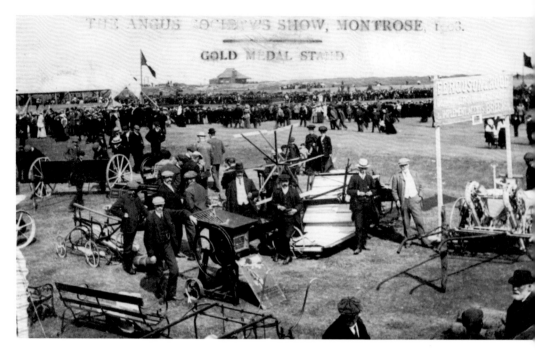

Angus Society Show and Proclamation of King George V

Agricultural shows were very popular in towns around Angus, being held in Forfar, Arbroath and Brechin. The postcard above is the Angus Society's Show in 1908, held on Montrose links. The beach pavilion can be seen in the background. This postcard was issued by Ferguson & Hood, Ironmongers, Brechin, and was probably used as an advertisement. The postcard below shows crowds gathering at the town square in the High Street to hear the proclamation of King George V, read on the death of Edward VII (6 May 1910).

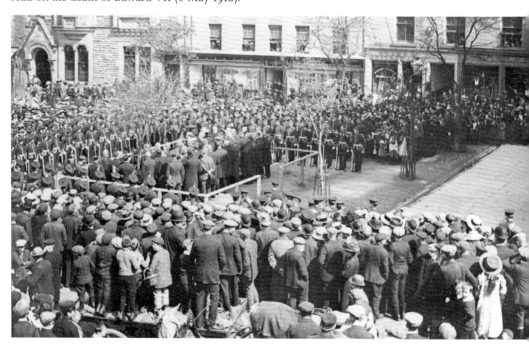

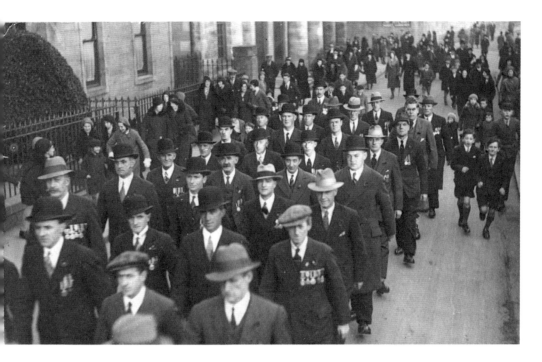

Remembrance Day Parade and Silver Jubilee Celebrations
The postcard above shows the Royal British Legion marching up John Street towards the High Street. This was probably a Remembrance Day parade through the town around 1925. The postcard below shows The Butts in Panmure Place decorated for the Silver Jubilee celebrations on 6 May 1935. This house remains exactly the same in structure apart from the iron railings, which were removed during the Second World War.

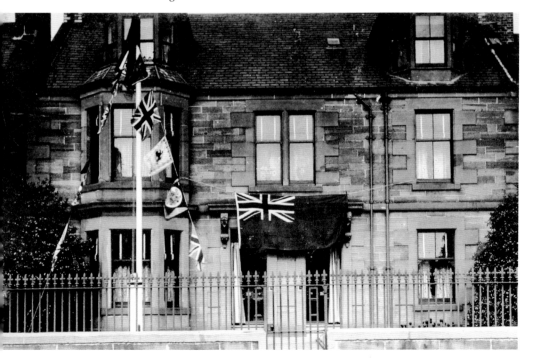

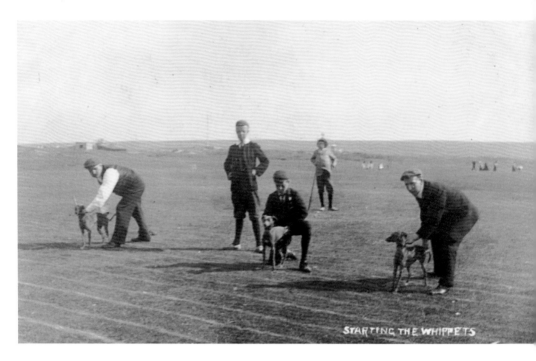

Starting the Whippets and Geo. St Helen's Entertainers
The postcard shows owners with their whippets on Montrose links. This postcard was published by J. G. Brown around 1908, and shows the whippets under training, ready for the start of a race. During the summer months, entertainers made regular appearances at Montrose links and local halls. Those included the Geisha Entertainers, Dave Summervill's Mascots and Fred Crompton's Entertainers, to name just a few. The postcard below shows Geo. St Helen's Entertainers in 1912.

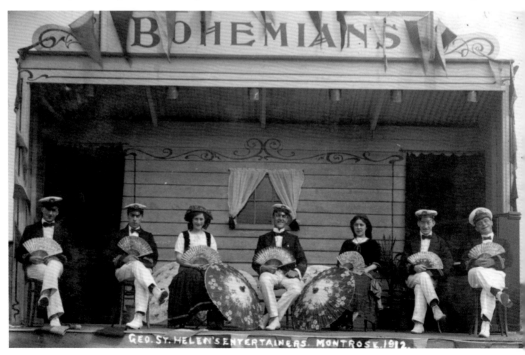

SECTION 4

BUILDINGS, BRIDGES
& MONUMENTS

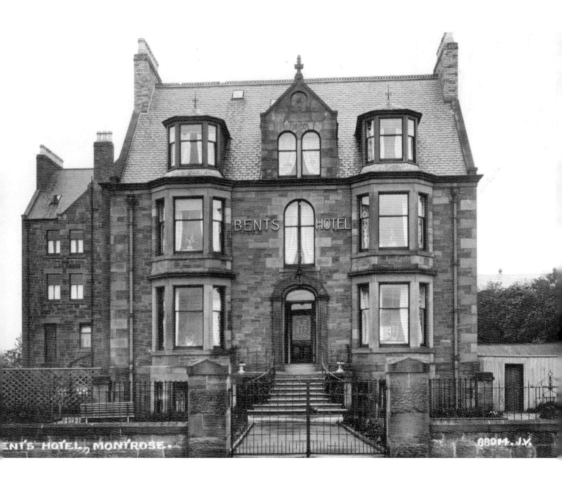

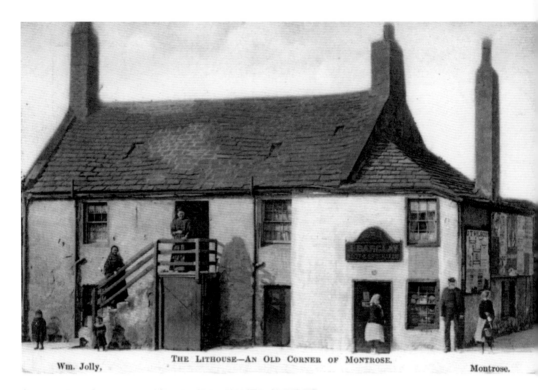

THE LITHOUSE—AN OLD CORNER OF MONTROSE.

Wm. Jolly,   Montrose.

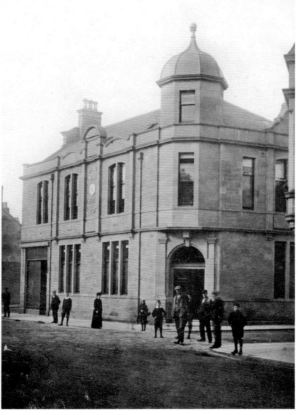

The Lithouse and YMCA Building
The Lithouse was situated at the corner of Murray Street and Lower Hall Street. The postcard above shows an early view of around 1904. It was erected towards the end of the seventeenth century on the croft of St John, the ground belonging to the Brethren of the Knights Templars of Jerusalem. In the early days, it was occupied by the Burgh Litster (or Dyer) and Inspector of the Linen Threads, which the town was once famous for making. The 'too-fa' on the right was for many years used as the collection house for the Petty Customs. The *c.* 1909 postcard on the left shows the new YMCA building that was built on the site.

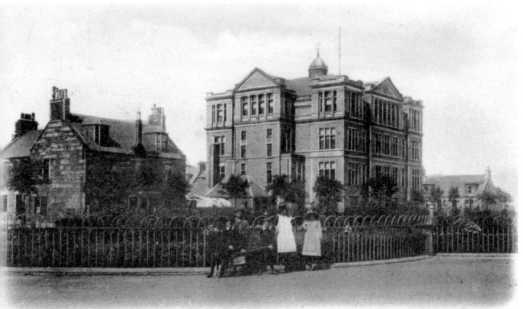

Links Street School, Montrose. RELIABLE SERIES.

North Links School and The Academy

The above postcard shows the south-east side of the North Links School around 1908. This was the only primary school in the district that had a swimming pool, and most children learned to swim there, including those from other primary schools. It was demolished in the early 1980s and sheltered housing built in its place. Montrose Academy's foundation stone was laid in 1815, and below is a postcard view of it around 1906, looking at the front and south side. This was Montrose's only senior school.

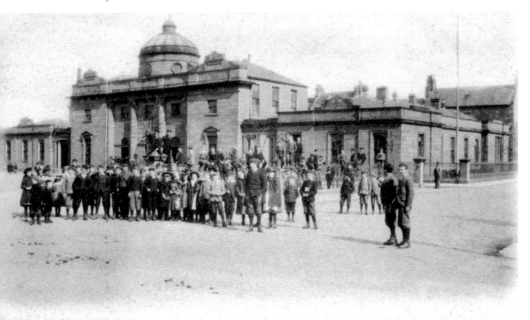

The Academy, Montrose. RELIABLE SERIES.

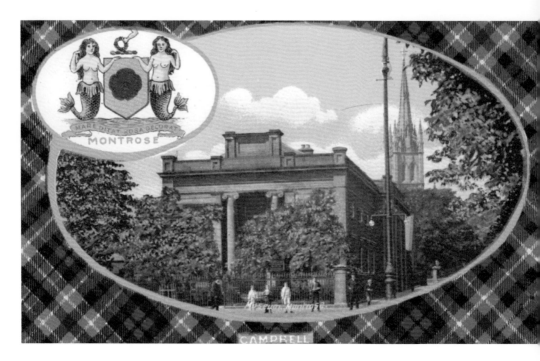

Montrose Museum and House of Refuge

The postcard of the Montrose Museum above was issued by the Tartan Border Series with the Montrose coat of arms. The museum is situated on the corner of Museum Street and Panmure Terrace. It was founded in 1839, opened in 1842 and extended in 1899. The postcard below shows the Dorward House of Refuge, which is situated near the top of Dorward Road, and was opened on 29 June 1839. William Dorward built and gifted this to the town. It is now called Dorward House and is a care home.

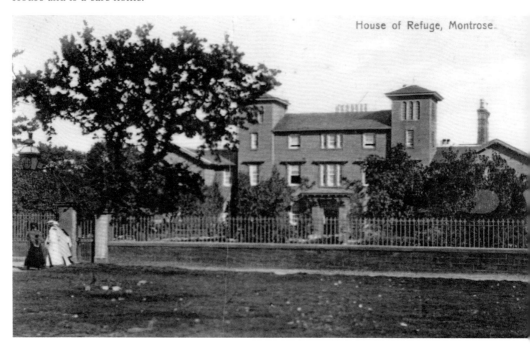

House of Refuge, Montrose.

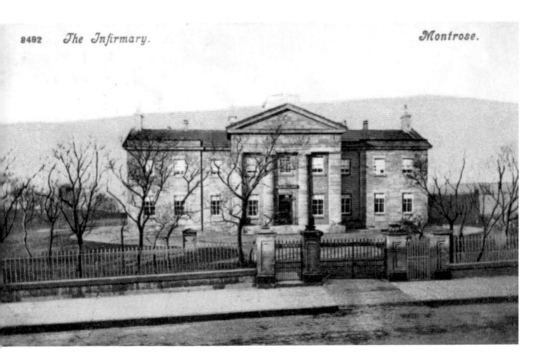

Montrose Infirmary and Montrose Library

The postcard above is a view of the Montrose Infirmary, situated near the bottom of Bridge Street. It was opened in 1839, and was extended in the late 1800s and the 1920s. A sun balcony was added to the upstairs ward in 1937. The postcard below is from the Tartan Border Series and shows the Montrose Library. It is situated at the junction of Castle Place, Castle Street and Bridge Street. It was built with the money from Andrew Carnegie and was opened by John Morley MP in 1905.

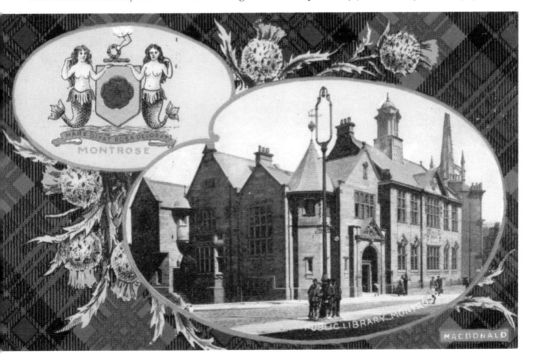

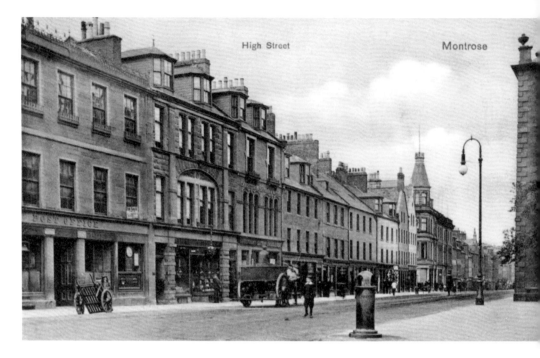

Post Office

Montrose has had a post office since before 1700, and it has been situated in several different locations over the years. The postcard above shows its location before 1907 when in the High Street opposite the church steeple. In 1907, it moved to Bridge Street and this view can be seen on the postcard below. It stayed in this location until 1993, when it moved back to the High Street, this time into the Co-op premises. The building in Bridge Street is still used as a sorting office and mail pick-up point.

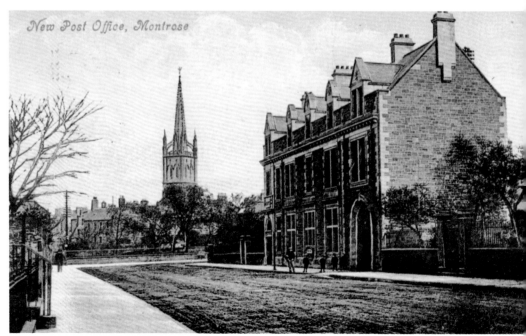

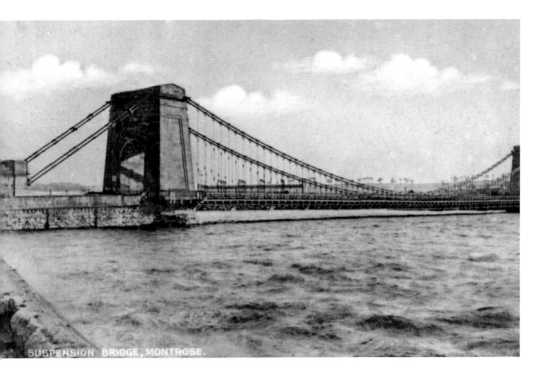

Suspension Bridge
The Montrose Suspension Bridge was opened in 1829 at a cost of £20,000, and replaced the old wooden bridge that was known as the 'Timer Brig'. The Suspension Bridge was 432 feet long and 26 feet wide. Here are two views of the bridge, the top postcard looking east and the postcard below is a view looking north through it from Rossie Island, showing the old toll house on the left.

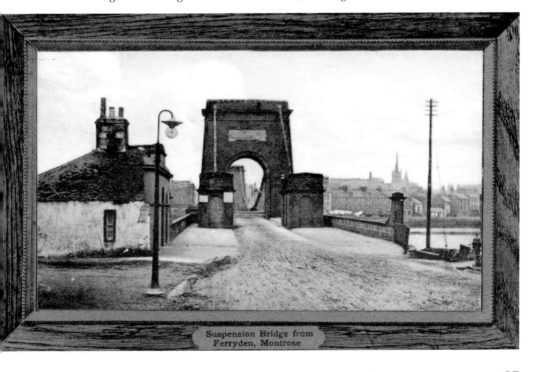

Suspension Bridge from Ferryden, Montrose

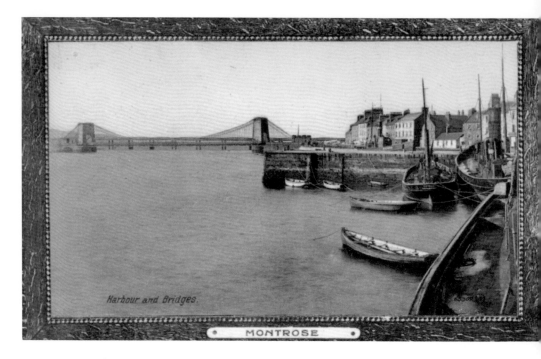

Harbour and Bridges.

MONTROSE

Suspension Bridge

Another view of the Suspension Bridge is shown in the postcard above, this time looking west from the harbour area with Wharf Street on the right. In 1832, the Suspension Bridge was damaged when gale-force winds tore up the roadway and, in 1880, seven people were killed when one of the chains gave way. Due to continual damage to its chains caused by bad weather, it was to demolished in 1930. The postcard below shows the balustrade from the Suspension Bridge re-erected in the grounds of the Montrose Museum.

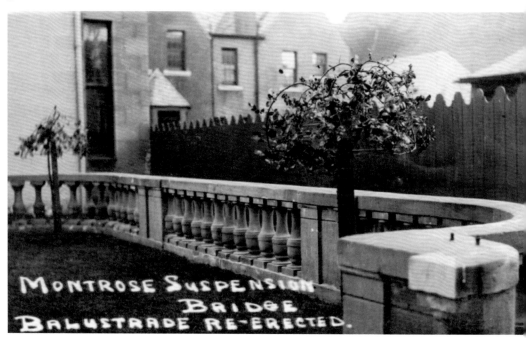

MONTROSE SUSPENSION BRIDGE BALUSTRADE RE-ERECTED.

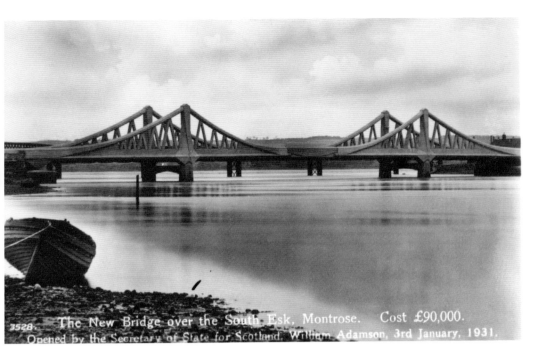

New Bridge

Here we have two views of the New Bridge, which replaced the Suspension Bridge; the top view is looking west and the bottom view is looking east. It was opened on 3 January 1931 by William Adamson and the cost of construction was £90,000. This was a cantilever bridge built from reinforced concrete and was the only one of its kind in the world. Due to the strain of modern traffic, it was demolished in 2004 and a replacement was built by 2005.

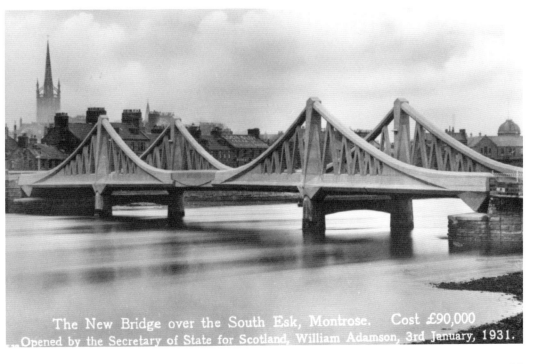

The New Bridge over the South Esk, Montrose. Cost £90,000
Opened by the Secretary of State for Scotland, William Adamson, 3rd January, 1931.

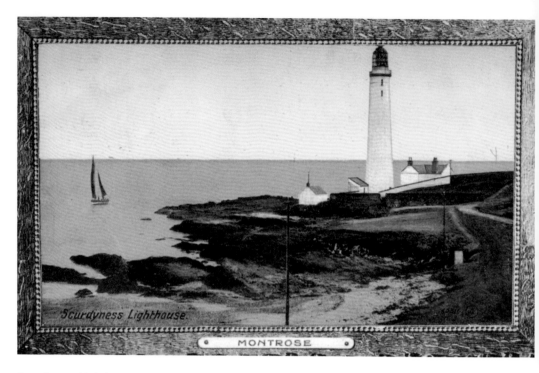

Scurdyness Lighthouse
Here are two views of Scurdyness Lighthouse from around 1910. This lighthouse is situated east of Ferryden village and access is by a single road, which makes a very nice walk in the summer time. It was first lit in 1870 and engineered by David and Thomas Stevenson. The lighthouse was automated in 1987.

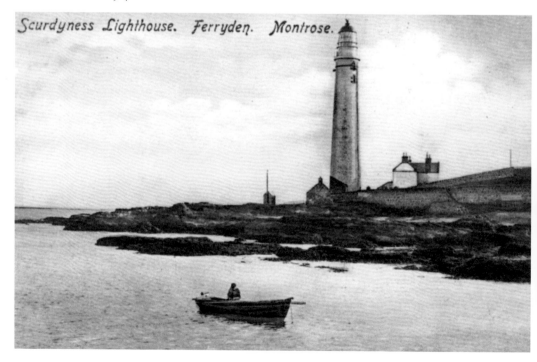

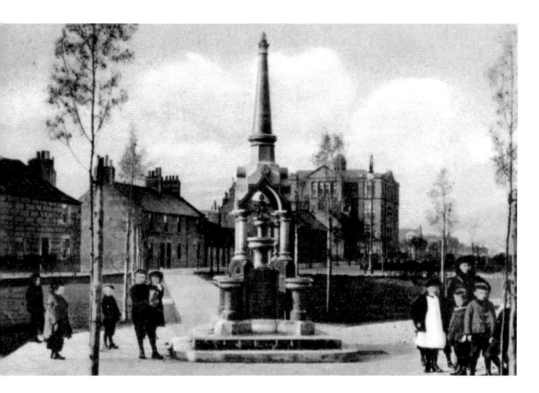

Jamieson Paton Fountain and Scott Memorial Fountain
The postcard above shows the Jamieson Paton Fountain in Jamieson Paton Park on the Mid Links. Completed in 1905, it was made of Rubislaw, Royal Blue, Banchory and Balmoral granite, had a spire resting on four columns, with a drinking fountain at the end of each. Inside the arches is an ornamental fountain. The postcard below shows the Scott Memorial Fountain, which can also be found on the Mid Links in Scott Park. This memorial fountain was unveiled in 1904.

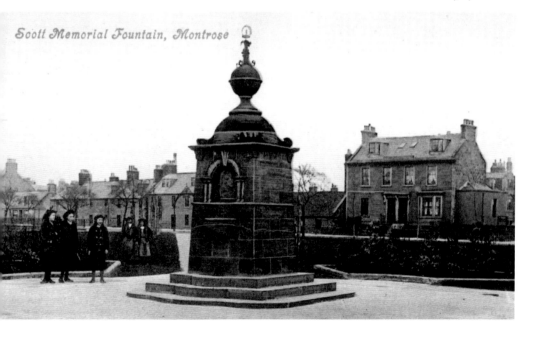

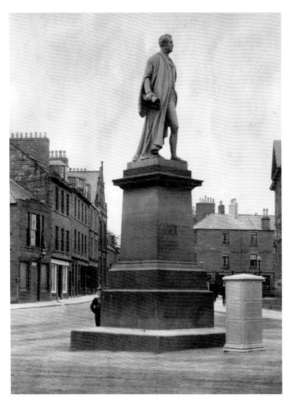

Monuments – Robert Peel and Joseph Hume

There are several monuments of famous people in Montrose. The postcard above shows one of Robert Peel, which can be found at the top of George Street in Peel Place. In 1822, he became home secretary, and introduced far-ranging criminal law and prison reform. He also created the Metropolitan Police. The terms 'bobbies' and 'peelers' came from his name. The postcard below shows the Joseph Hume monument, which can be found in the centre of the High Street opposite the top of Hume Street. Joseph Hume was a Scottish doctor and radical MP who was born in Montrose in 1777.

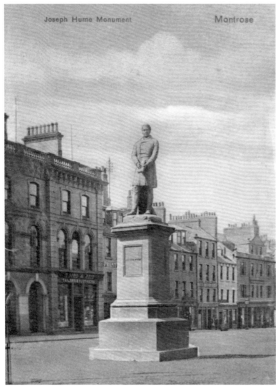

Joseph Hume Monument   Montrose

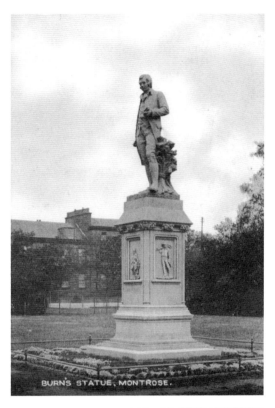

BURNS STATUE, MONTROSE.

Monuments – Robert Burns

The two postcards on this page are of the
Robert Burns statue in the Mid Links,
which was unveiled by Andrew Carnegie
in 1912. Robert Burns was Scotland's
greatest poet, and the statue was paid
for mainly by private subscription and
fundraising. Money left over from the
fund was used to clean the gravestones of
Burn's forebears in Glenbervie churchyard,
and to place a brass plate on the house
at Bow Butts, where Burns had stayed
overnight with his cousin, James Burnes.

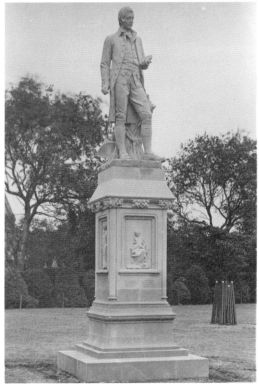

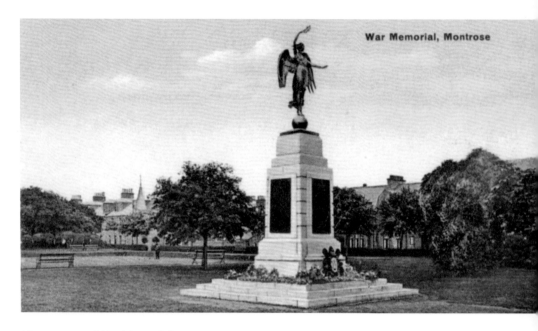

War Memorial, Montrose

Monuments – War Memorial

The two postcards on this page are of the war memorial in the Mid Links. The memorial's central structure commemorates the fallen of the First World War, and was unveiled in 1924. The unveiling attracted 3,000–4,000 people, and many wreaths from private individuals and associations were laid. At the end of the Second World War, communities had the choice of either erecting a new war memorial or adapting the existing one. The latter was chosen and was designed and sculpted by William Lamb, a local sculptor, and cast by George Mancini, probably the finest bronze founder of the twentieth century. The 1939–45 war memorial was unveiled and dedicated at the Remembrance Day service in 1949, which again attracted a large attendance.

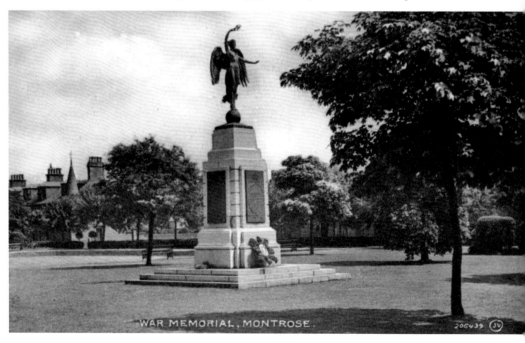

WAR MEMORIAL, MONTROSE.

SECTION 5
SPORT

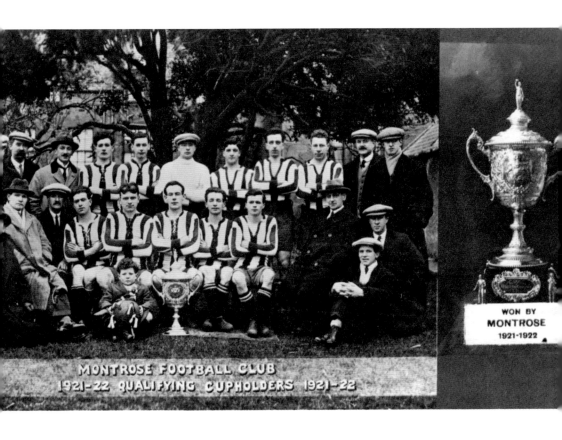

MONTROSE FOOTBALL CLUB
1921-22 QUALIFYING CUPHOLDERS 1921-22

WON BY
MONTROSE
1921-1922

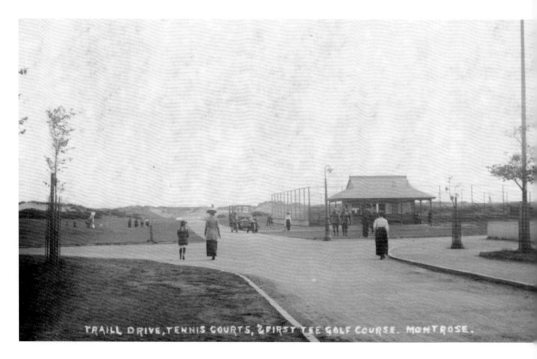

TRAILL DRIVE, TENNIS COURTS, & FIRST TEE GOLF COURSE. MONTROSE.

Tennis Courts

The postcard above shows the original tennis courts when they were on the links at the north end of the Traill Drive. Those courts opened in 1912 and closed in 1932. Also seen is the first tee at the golf course. On the postcard below are the new tennis courts situated between Warrack Terrace and Dorward Place. It moved from the links after it closed in 1932. This view was photographed from the North Links School.

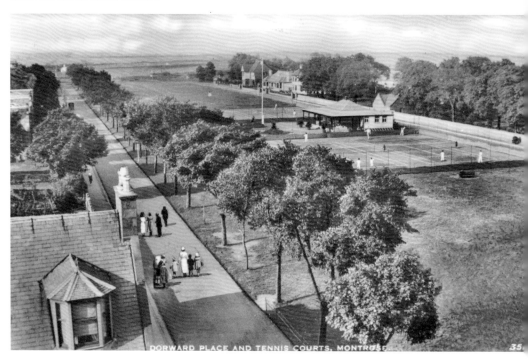

DORWARD PLACE AND TENNIS COURTS, MONTROSE. 35.

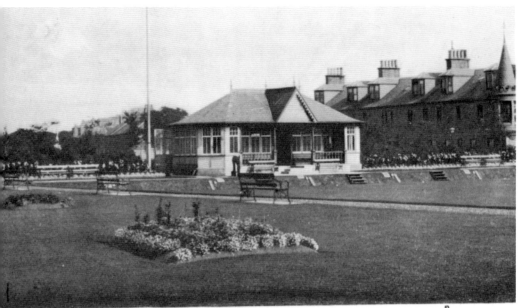

Bowling Greens

The postcard above shows the Hope Paton Bowling Green on the Mid Links. Along with the Hope Paton Gardens, it was formally opened on 31 August 1904. There was a large turn out of local people, representing a cross section of all the social and political groups in the area. The postcard below shows the Melville Bowling Green at Melville Gardens on the Mid Links. It was formally opened by Provost Milne on 5 June 1878. The Melville Gardens were opened on 1 September 1876 and the event lasted two days.

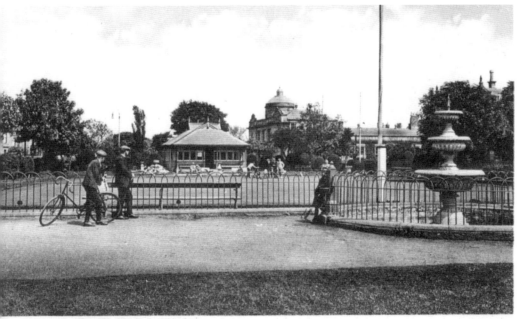

MELVILLE BOWLING GREEN, MONTROSE.

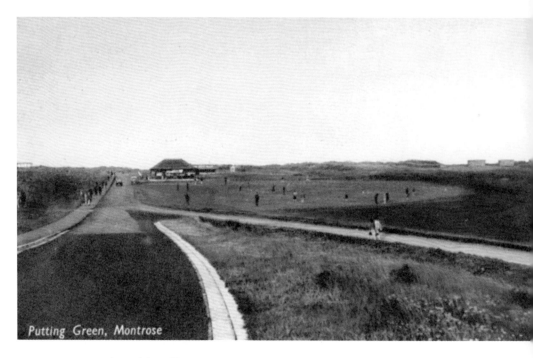

Putting Green, Montrose

Putting Green and Medal Golf Course

The game of putting was very popular with holidaymakers and locals alike. This putting green on the postcard above was situated at the south end of the Traill Drive; a caravan site now occupies this site. The postcard below shows the first tee at the Montrose Medal Golf Course. The golf clubhouses behind are the Royal Albert Golf Club and the Victoria Golf Club, and Grey Harlings house is on the right. In 1986, these two golf clubs amalgamated to form the Royal Montrose Golf Club.

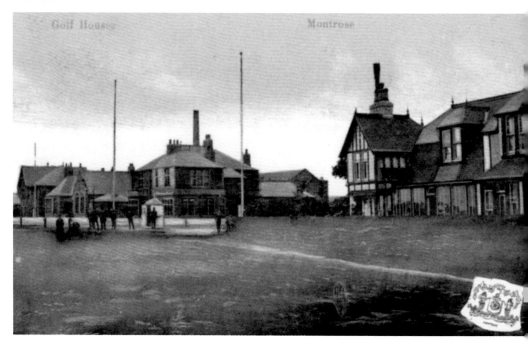

SECTION 6
MILITARY

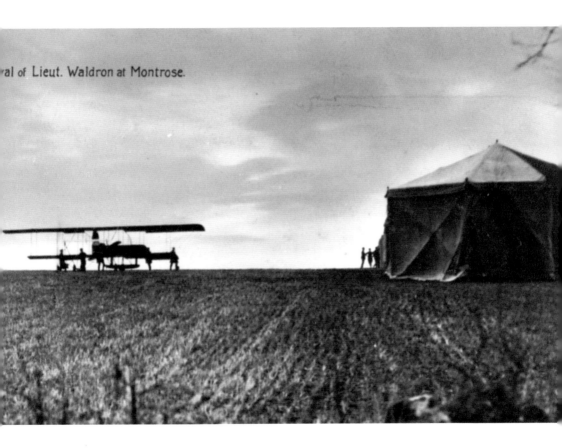

al of Lieut. Waldron at Montrose.

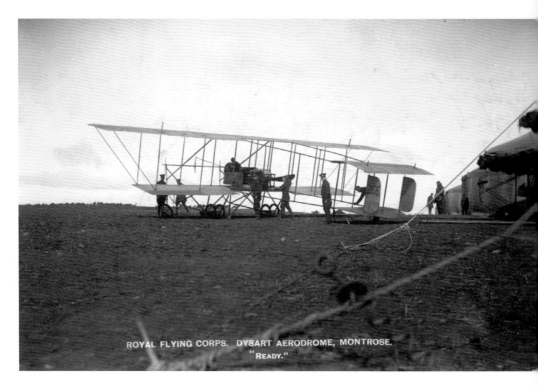

ROYAL FLYING CORPS. DYSART AERODROME, MONTROSE.
"READY."

Dysart Aerodrome

These two postcards show aircraft at their tented hangers at Upper Dysart Farm. The top postcard shows an aircraft preparing for a flight, while the bottom postcard shows an aircraft tuning up.

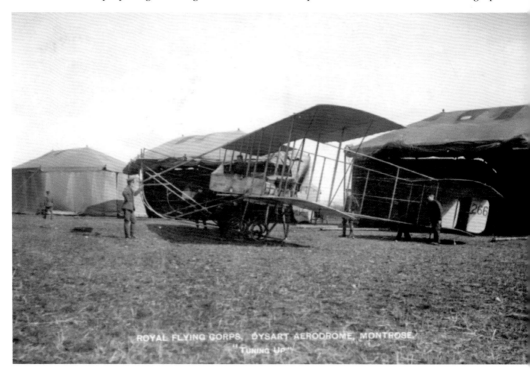

ROYAL FLYING CORPS. DYSART AERODROME, MONTROSE.
"TUNING UP"

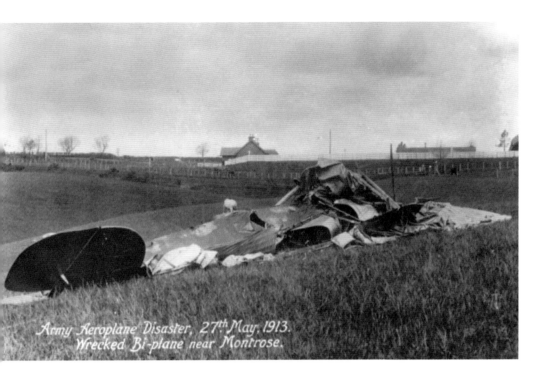

Army Aeroplane Disaster, 27th May, 1913. Wrecked Bi-plane near Montrose.

Aeroplane Disaster, 1913

On 27 May 1913, while out on a practice flight, Lt Desmond Arthur's aircraft crashed in a field at Lunan, which was not far from Dysart Farm, and was killed. The postcard above shows his wrecked plane in the field at Lunan. The postcard below shows his funeral on its way to St Mary's Episcopal church, from there he was taken to Sleepyhillock Cemetery for burial.

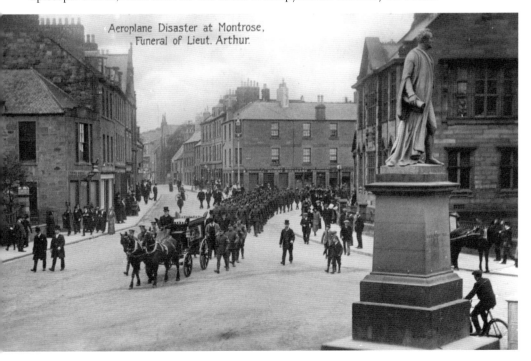

Aeroplane Disaster at Montrose, Funeral of Lieut. Arthur.

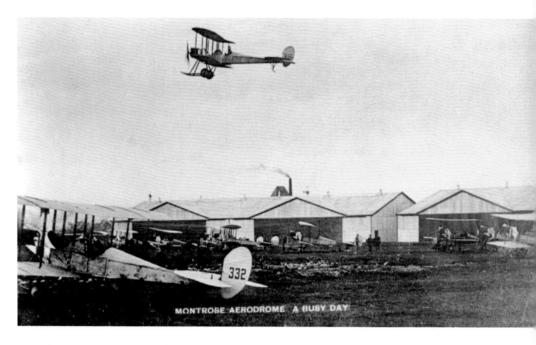

MONTROSE AERODROME A BUSY DAY

Montrose Aerodrome and Hillside

After surveying the area and not considering the airfield site ideal, Maj. Burke gained agreement to move the base to Broomfield Farm, just north of the town. At the end of 1913, Army engineers erected three hangers on the site (known as 'Major Burke's Sheds'), enabling the squadron to move there in the beginning of 1914. The postcard above shows the airfield and hangers at Broomfield on a busy day. The postcard below shows an aeroplane in a field at the village of Hillside, not far from Broomfield. The story goes that this aeroplane overshot the airfield at Broomfield and had to land here due to a shortage of fuel.

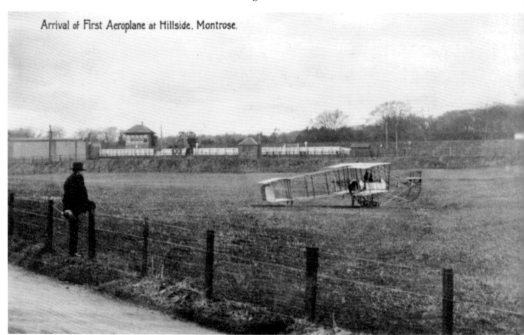

Arrival of First Aeroplane at Hillside, Montrose.

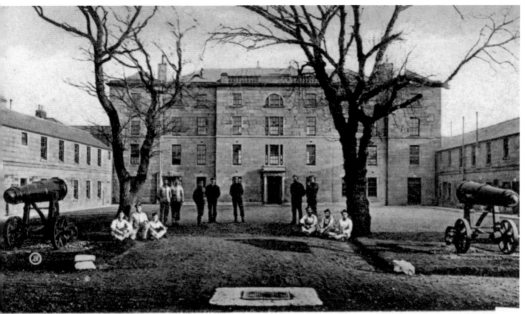

The Barracks, Montrose   Valentines Series   44757

Barracks in the South Links and Union Mill Barracks
The above postcard shows the military barracks in the South Links, near the docks. This was the first lunatic asylum in Scotland, which was instituted in 1782. After this asylum closed and moved to Hillside in 1857, the building lay empty for a number of years. In the early 1900s, the military took the building over as their barracks. The postcard below shows soldiers at Union Mill Barracks who were drafted for France in 1917. Most military personnel stationed here were from the USA, and quite a few of them went down with 'Spanish Flu'. Squadrons that were stationed at Union Mills were the 41st and the 138st Aero Squadrons, to name a few.

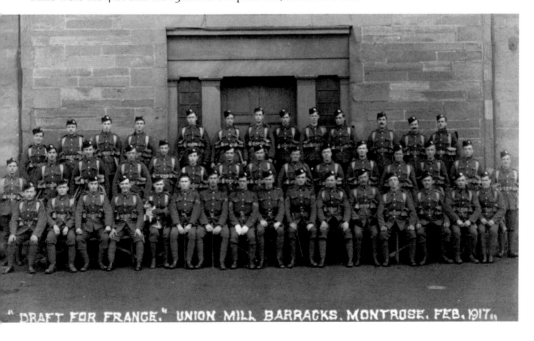

"DRAFT FOR FRANCE." UNION MILL BARRACKS, MONTROSE, FEB. 1917.

53

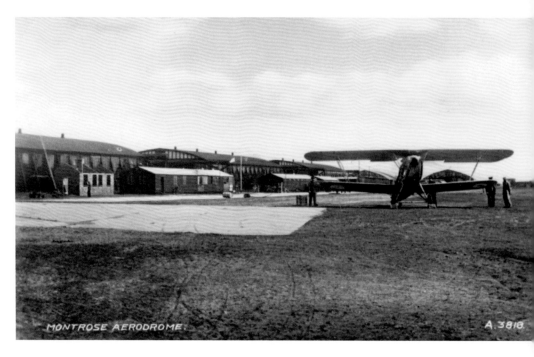

Broomfield Airfield

The two postcards here show Broomfield Airfield around 1936–38. After the First World War, Montrose Airfield closed its doors in 1920. Then, in 1930, the airfield returned to life, as it prepared to take on its new role as a training school. With the expansion scheme under way in the mid-1930s, Montrose Aerodrome opened early in 1936 as No. 8 Flying Training School. With the runways and hangers already in place, all the site needed was a dust off before it was ready to resume active service.

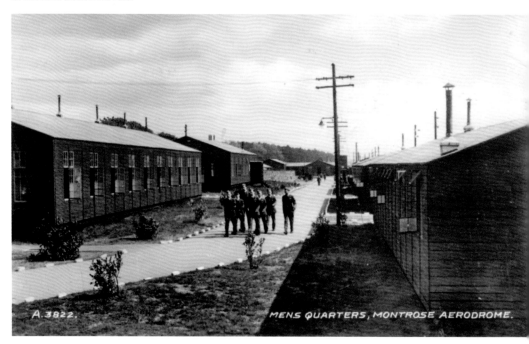

SECTION 7
THE BEACH & LINKS

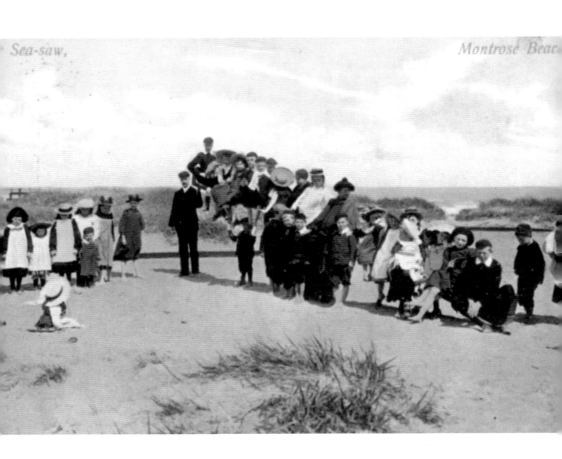

Sea-saw, Montrose Beac

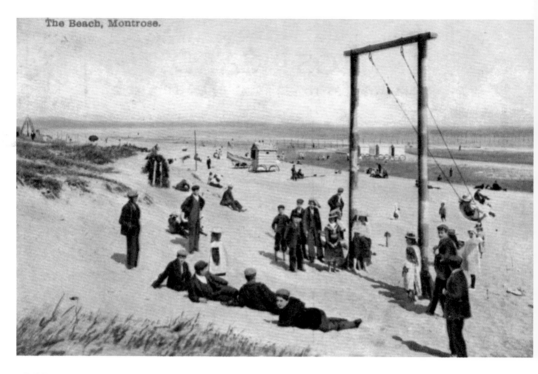

Children on the Beach

The beach and links have always been a popular attraction for holidaymakers at Montrose. These two postcards show children enjoying themselves at the swings on the beach. The changing huts on large metal wheels can be seen in the background.

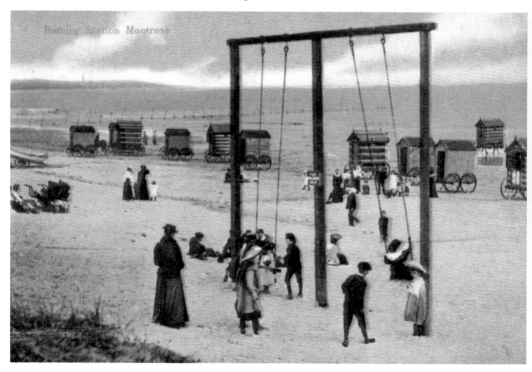

Bathing Station Montrose

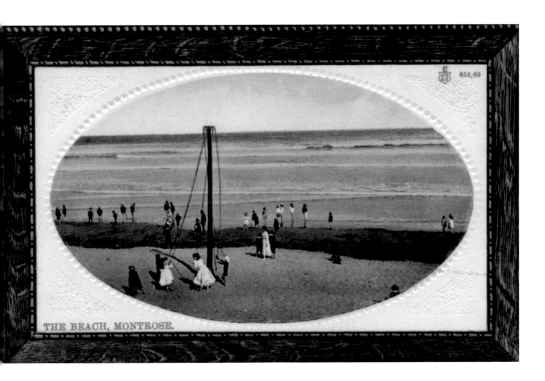

THE BEACH, MONTROSE.

The Maypole

The maypole was another great attraction for the children. Here we have two postcards showing children enjoying themselves on it. The postcard above shows the maypole down on the beach and the postcard below shows the other up on the roadside, the beach and Traill Pavilion in the background.

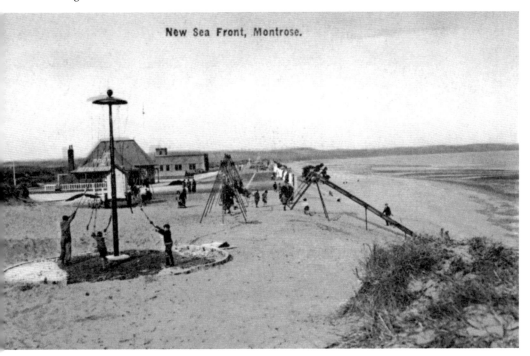

New Sea Front, Montrose.

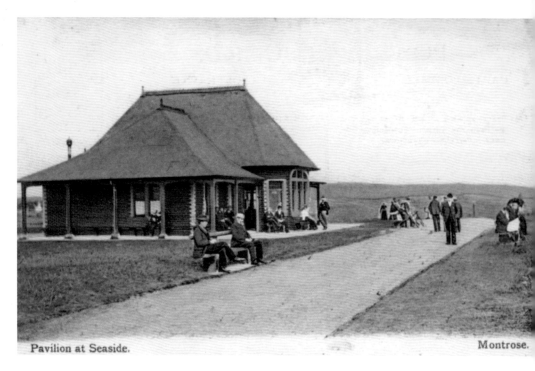

Pavilion at Seaside.   Montrose.

Beach Pavilion

Two views of the Beach Pavilion at the waterfront. The postcard above was taken before the Traill Pavilion was built in 1913, while the postcard below shows the Traill Pavilion in the background after completion.

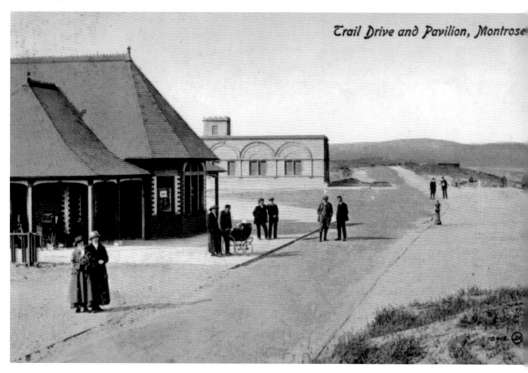

Trail Drive and Pavilion, Montrose

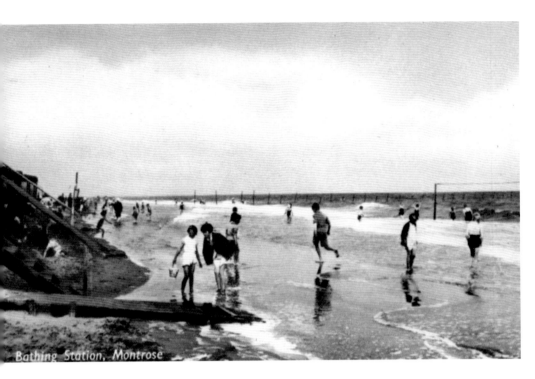

Montrose Beach, Looking North
Two postcards showing Montrose Beach looking north, where everyone seems to be enjoying themselves in the sun and sea waves.

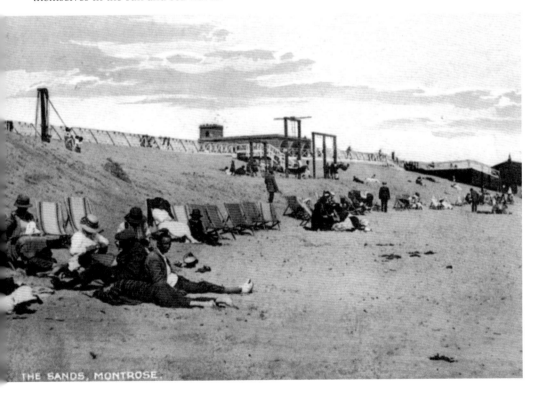

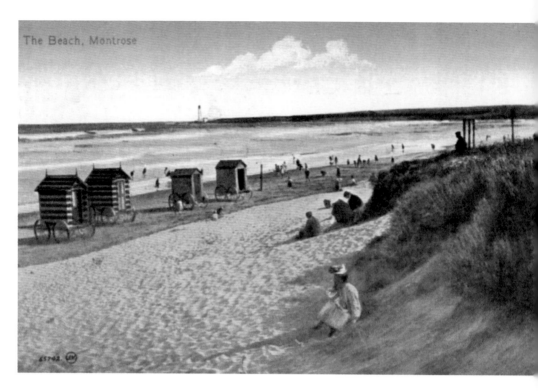

The Beach, Montrose

Montrose Beach, Looking South-East
Two postcards showing Montrose Beach looking south-east, with the top postcard showing Scurdyness Lighthouse in the background. The postcard below shows the Edwardian changing huts.

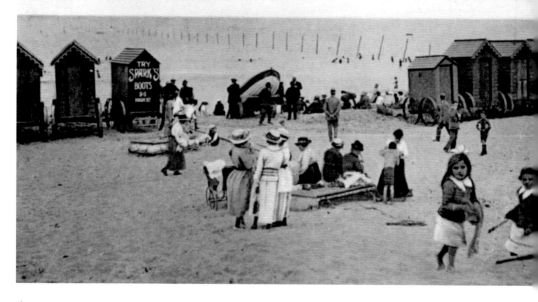

At the Seaside, Montrose

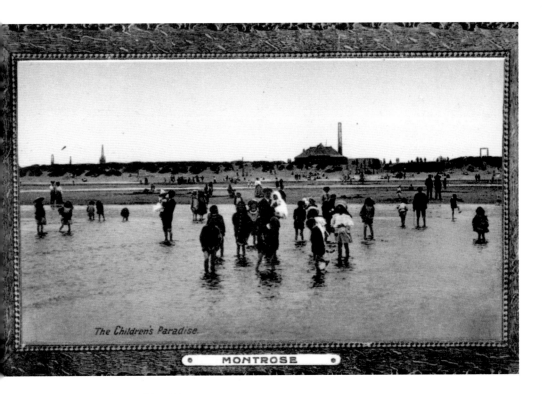

The Children's Paradise.

MONTROSE

Montrose Beach, Looking West

This two postcards shows views looking west towards the pavilions. At low tide, large, shallow pools were left on the beach, which children used as a safe bathing area.

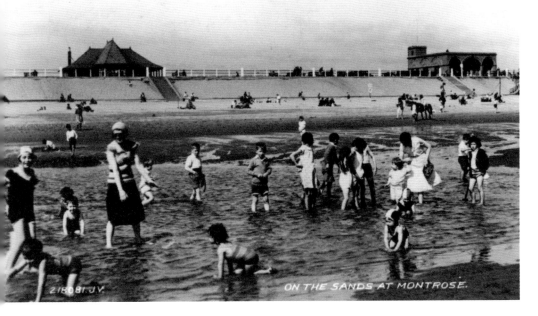

ON THE SANDS AT MONTROSE.

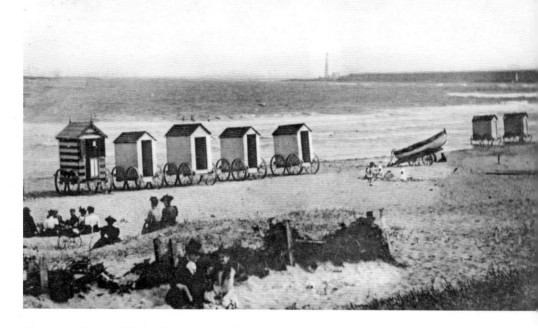

Bathing Station. Montrose.

Changing Huts and Trips Along the Beach

This view looking towards Scurdyness Lighthouse shows the swimmers' changing huts, which were on wheels so they could be moved about on the beach. More recently, one of those wheels was discovered on the beach by a local walker. It was donated to Montrose Museum. Donkey riding was another popular attraction at Montrose Beach. The postcard below shows children and adults alike enjoying the trips along the beach.

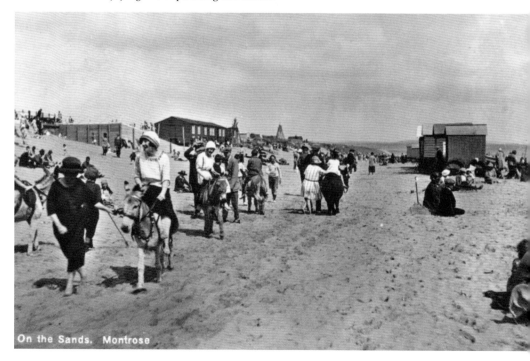

On the Sands. Montrose

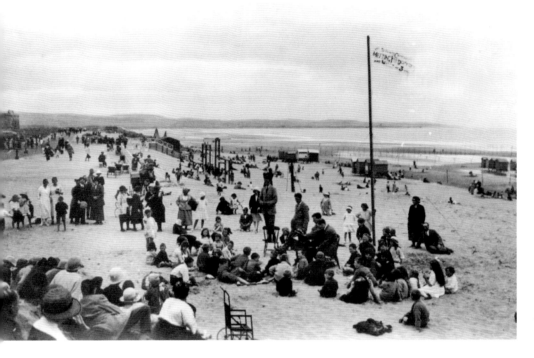

Students' Campaign and the Pierrots

The postcard above shows a students' campaign meeting for boys and girls being held on the beach, with a number of adults looking on. The postcard below shows children and adults being entertained by the Pierrots on the links. They were regular visitors to Montrose in the summer months.

The Pierots, Montrose

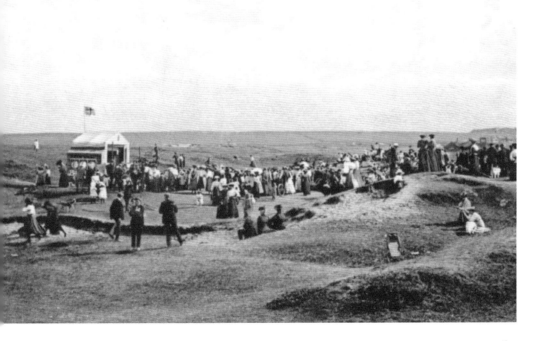

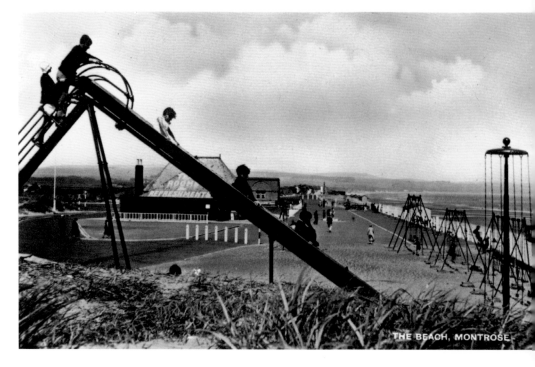

The Beach, Montrose

Amusements

The postcard above shows a close up view of the chute, swings and maypole at the beach roadside. Later, those amusements were moved to the area behind the Beach Pavilion, which can be seen in the postcard below.

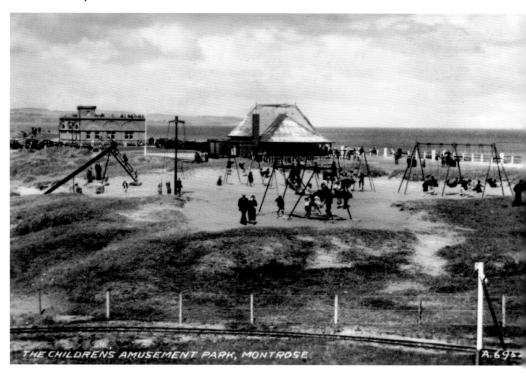

THE CHILDREN'S AMUSEMENT PARK, MONTROSE.   A.695

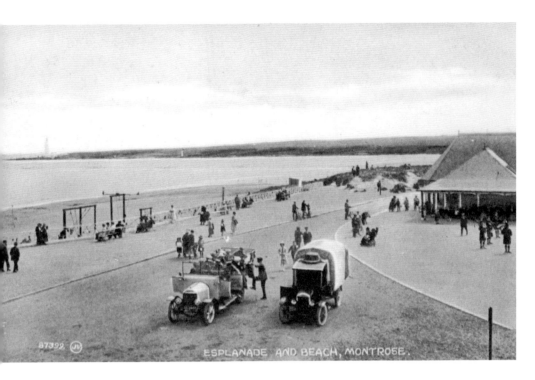

Esplanade and Beach

The postcard above shows a *c.* 1920 view of the esplanade and beach, with the pavilion on the right. An early-style bus is picking up passengers who were probably going back into the town. The postcard below shows the same view around twenty years later, where you can see the style of vehicles have changed.

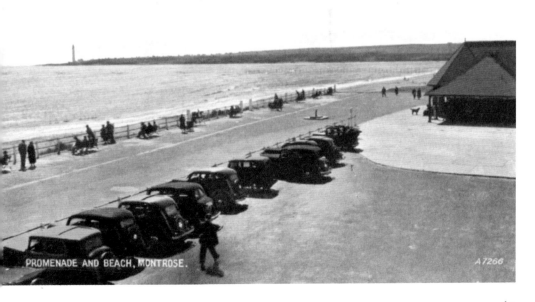

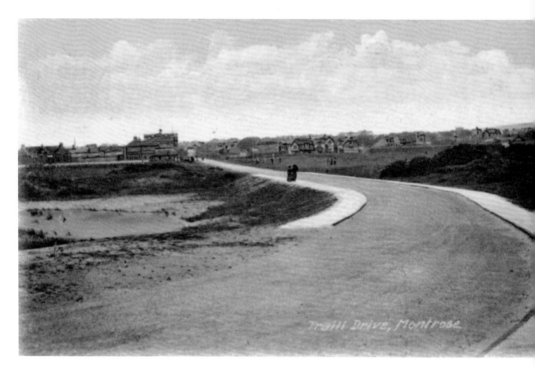

The Traill Drive

The top postcard shows an early view of the north end of the Traill Drive looking west, with the North Links School in the background. The postcard below shows the north end of the Traill Drive looking east.

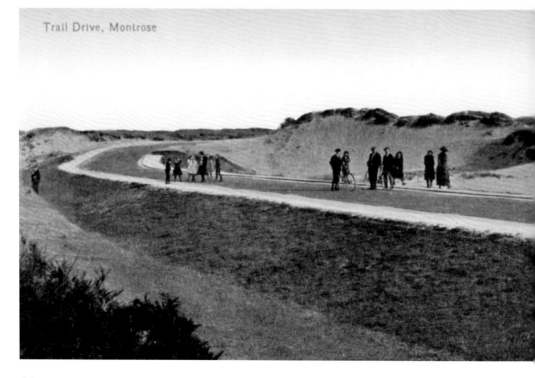

FERRYDEN & USAN

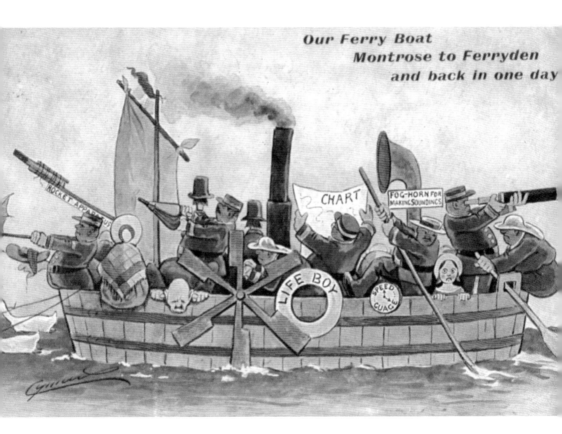

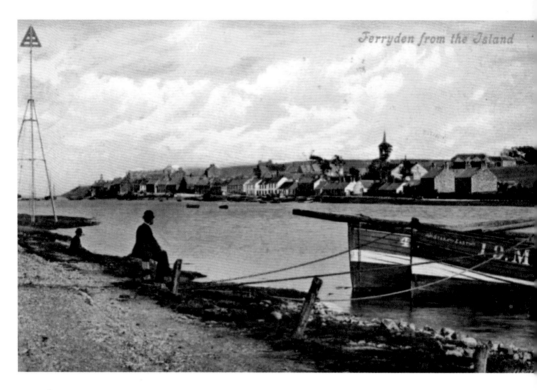

Ferryden
Two postcard views looking from Rossie Island across to Ferryden. This estuary of the River South Esk was reclaimed and the Sea Oil Support Base was built here in the 1970s.

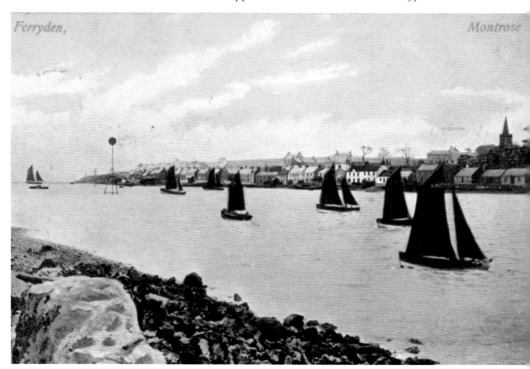

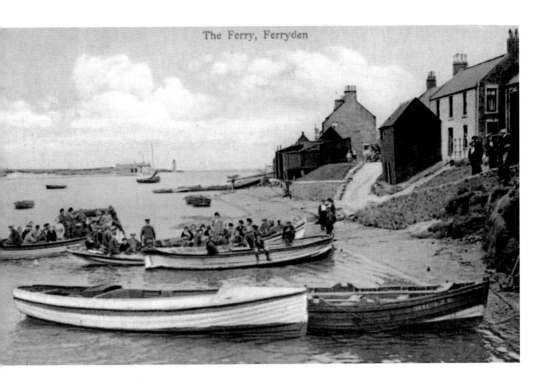

Ferry Boats at Ferryden Beach

Two postcard views of the ferry boats at Ferryden Beach. The ferry boat would mostly take women who worked in the mills at Montrose across the estuary of the River South Esk. The Esk Hotel can be seen on the right of the postcard above and the shed in front of it was used for storing its beer.

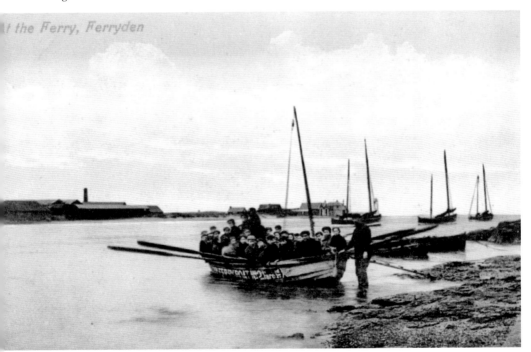

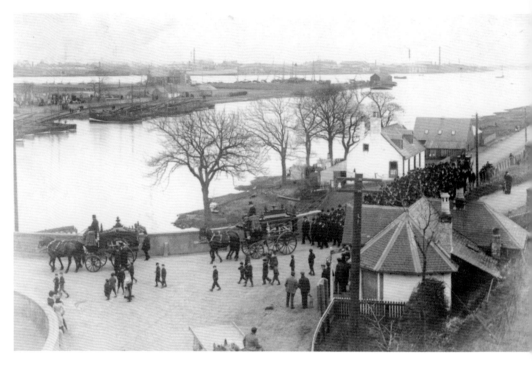

Funeral Leaving Ferryden and Rossie Island Cemetery

In April 1906, two Ferryden fishermen, Charles Anderson and Alexander Pert, were killed on the fishing vessel *Betty Inglis* after they were struck by a broken mast. The postcard above shows the funeral leaving Ferryden and about to cross the Inch Bridge, and below is a view of the funeral in Rossie Island Cemetery.

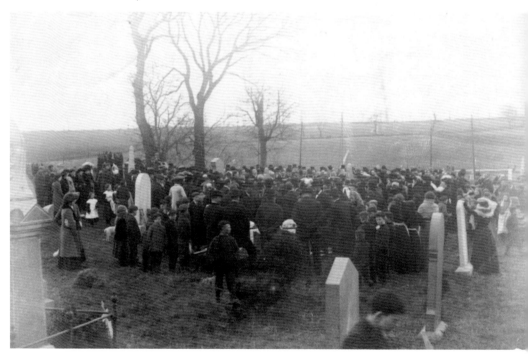

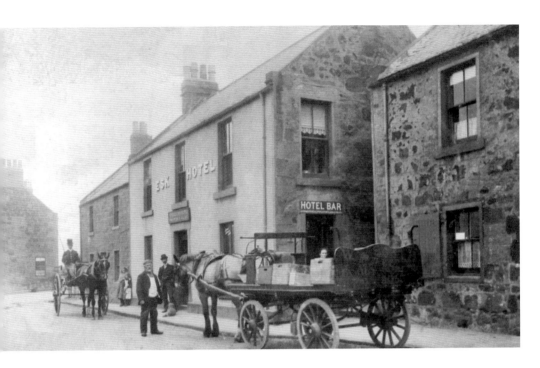

Esk Hotel and View from the Beach

The postcard above shows Ferryden's only hotel, the Esk Hotel. A horse and cart is at the door with a delivery of drinks. For generations, the Calder family ran this hotel and, in the 1920s, it was the village's only pub. The view below is looking up from the beach towards the General Merchant Store, run by William Findlay, and the post office on the left, run by Jim West. The church hall can just be seen on the right.

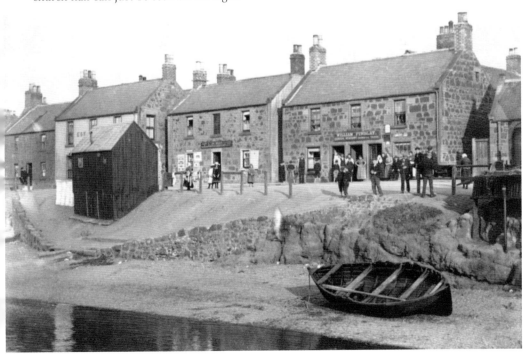

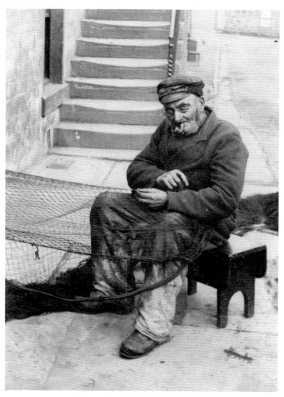

Fishermen

All fishermen did not go out to sea. Some stayed at home to support the work in making and repairing fishing nets, gutting fish and preparing bait. These two postcards show one fisherman at Rossie Square mending nets and another on the beach cleaning fish.

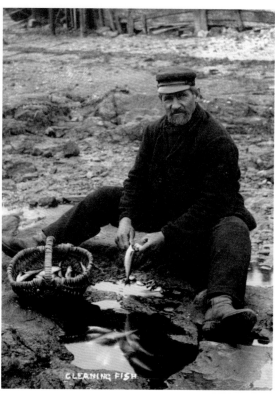

CLEANING FISH

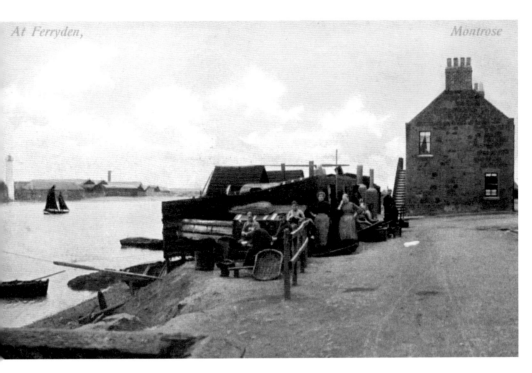

Women at Work

Local women who did not work in the Montrose mills also helped in repairing or making fishing nets. The top postcard shows women at work in Brownlow Place. The postcard below shows maintenance work on a creel boat on the beach in front of Brownlow Place.

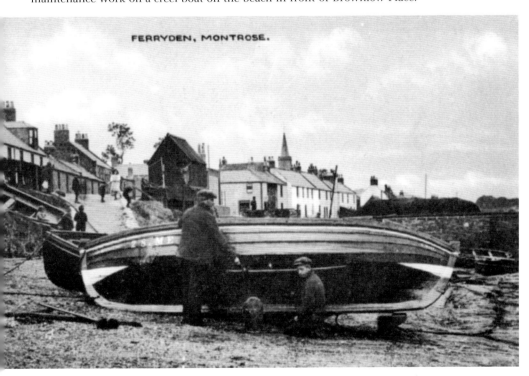

FERRYDEN, MONTROSE.

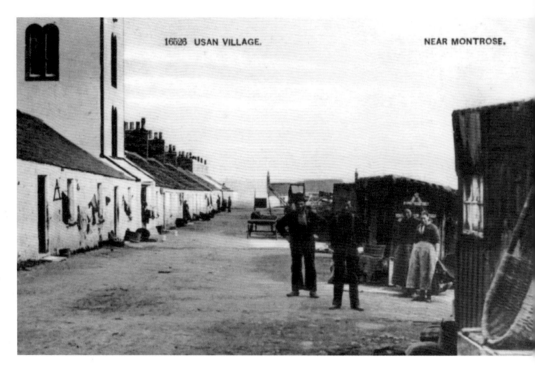

Usan

A further mile south of Ferryden you find the old fishing village of Usan. On these two postcards, we see the row of cottages that housed families in the early 1900s. The top postcard is a view looking east, and the postcard below is a view looking west. The cottages are now in ruins.

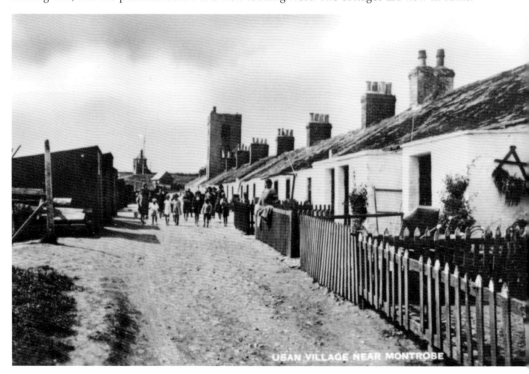

USAN VILLAGE NEAR MONTROSE

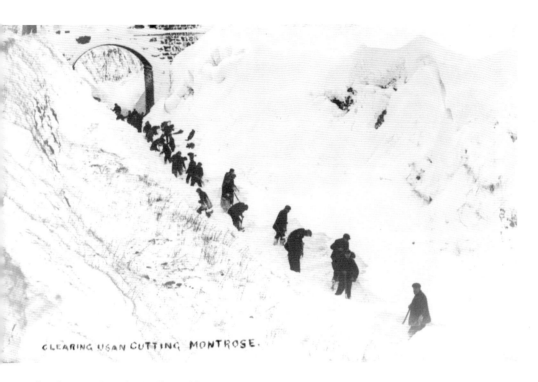

CLEARING USAN CUTTING MONTROSE.

Aberdeen to Dundee Railway Line
The main Aberdeen to Dundee railway line ran past Usan village. During the bad snowstorms of the early 1900s, this railway cutting got regularly blocked. These two postcards show workers manually digging and clearing the snow, and a railway engine stuck in the snow.

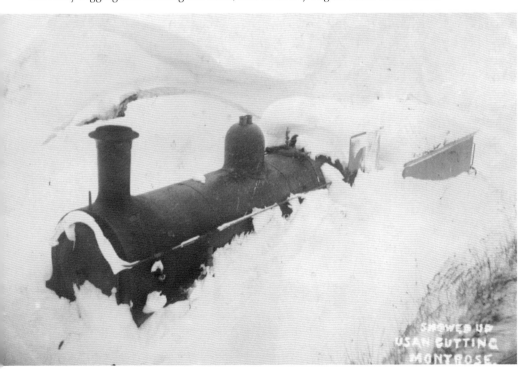

SNOWED UP
USAN CUTTING
MONTROSE.

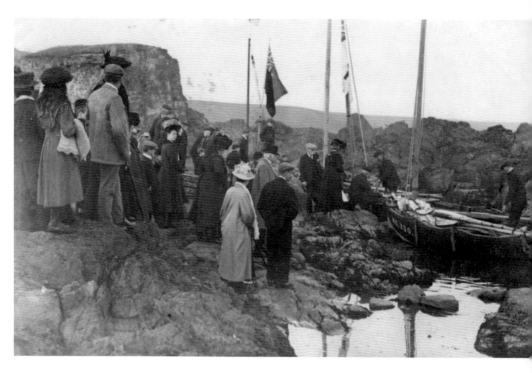

Boat 'Christening'

Here we have two postcard views of christaning boats at Usan, near the old saltworks, around 1905. The small boats have decorated masts and were used for sma'line and creel fishing. They were probably built at Montrose.

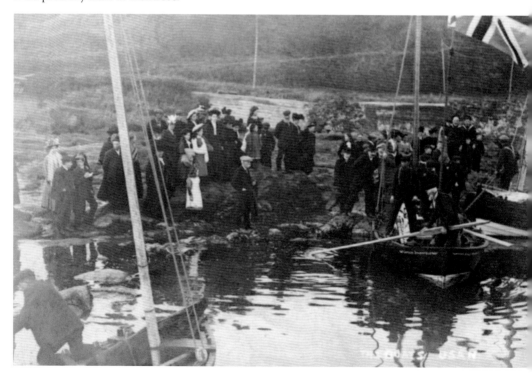

SECTION 9
HILLSIDE & CRAIGO

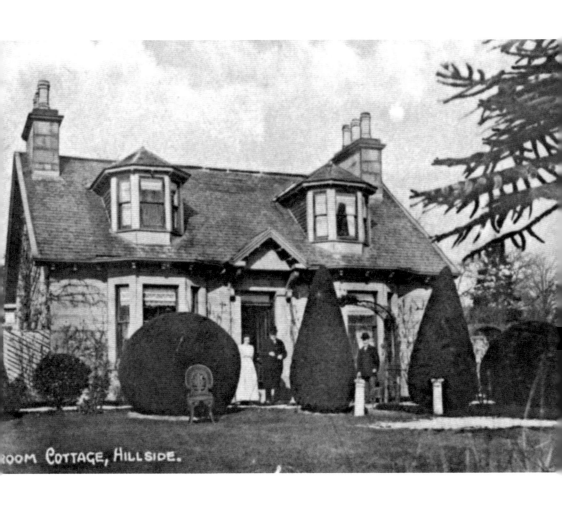

ROOM COTTAGE, HILLSIDE.

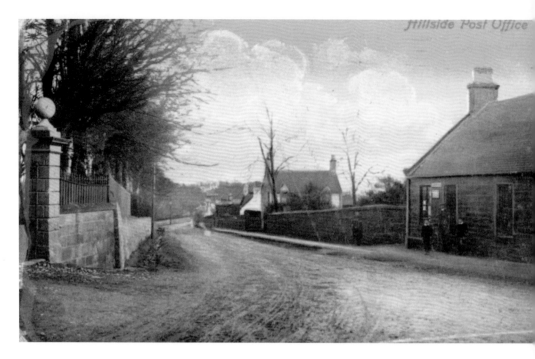

Hillside Post Office and Railway Station

Hillside village is found about 1 mile north of Montrose. The village has had a post office since 1847, and the postcard above shows a *c.* 1906 view of it when it was situated at the top of Main Road. The present location of the post office is at the bottom of this road. The postcard below shows a snow-covered railway station (North British) at Hillside. It was situated at the right-hand side of the Hillside–Craigo road, and closed in 1927.

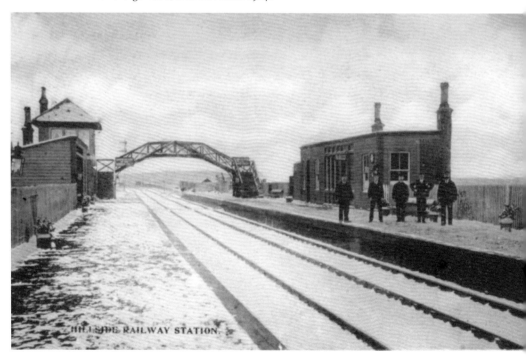

HILLSIDE RAILWAY STATION.

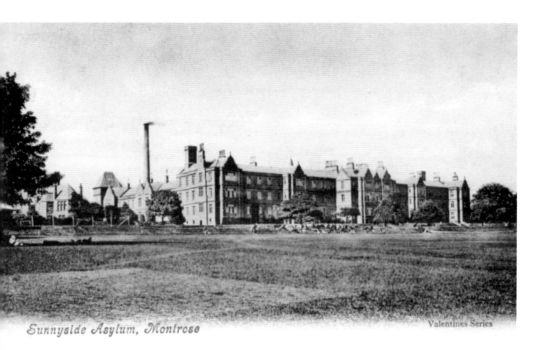

Sunnyside Asylum, Montrose

Valentines Series

Sunnyside Royal Asylum

Up until 1781, the mentally insane were kept alongside ordinary prisoners in the tollbooth, which was located in the south end of the High Street in Montrose. On 6 May 1781, a new asylum opened on the South Links close to the docks. Then, in 1858, Sunnyside Royal Asylum at Hillside was opened. The postcard above shows a view of the asylum around 1908, and the postcard below shows staff at the front door of the main building on a sports day in 1915.

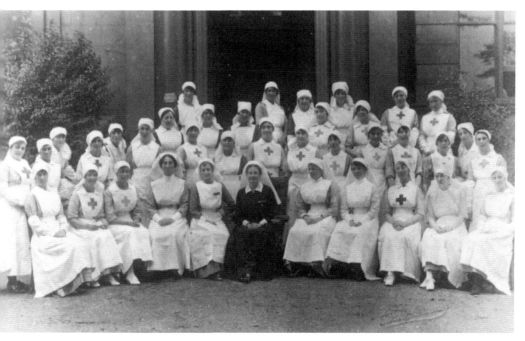

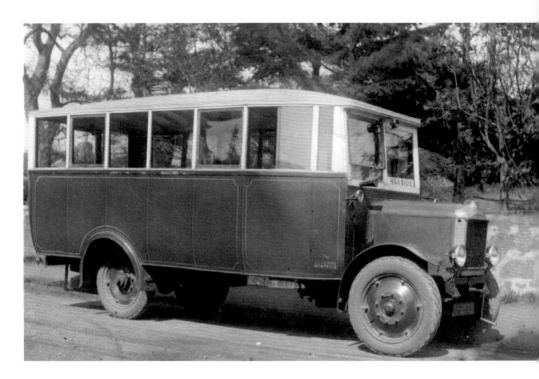

Hillside Bus Service and Temperance Hotel

There has always been a regular bus service between Hillside village and Montrose, and this postcard above shows a *c.* 1920 bus owned by J. B. Cairns, Montrose. The postcard below was photographed from the railway bridge and shows the Temperance Hotel and Roberts' general merchants store.

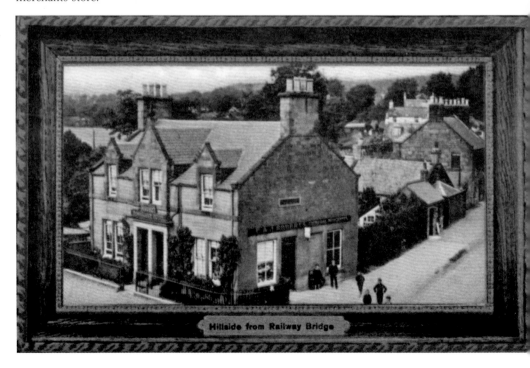

Hillside from Railway Bridge

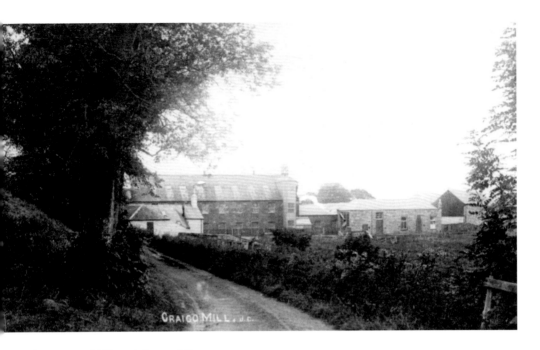

Craigo Jute Mill and General Store

A few miles further north lies the village of Craigo, which once had a busy jute mill, shown in the postcard above. It was originally owned by Richards from Aberdeen in the nineteenth century, and then sold to J. & D. Wilkie of Kirriemuir in 1868. It remained with them until it closed in 1987. This postcard was photographed around 1906 by J. Carr, a local Montrose photographer. The general store that served Craigo is shown in the postcard below, and was situated on the Hillside–Craigo road. At one point, this store also housed the Craigo post office until its closure in 1984. This building is now a private house.

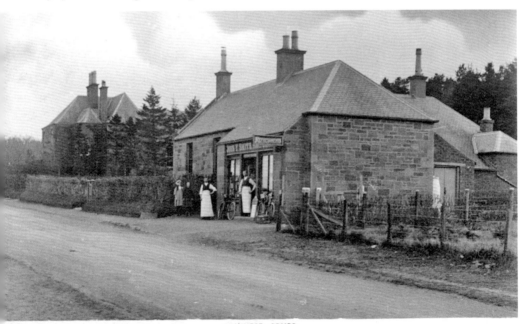

LOANHEAD, CRAIGO

81

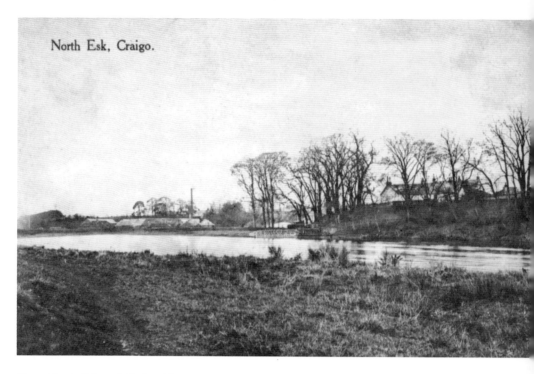

North Esk, Craigo.

River North Esk and Craigo House

The River North Esk, flowing past Craigo, is shown in the postcard above. It is a famous 35-mile-long salmon fishing river, and forms the boundary between Angus and Aberdeenshire at certain stages in its course. The now demolished Craigo House, shown on the postcard below, was the seat of the Carnegies and was situated south of Craigo village.

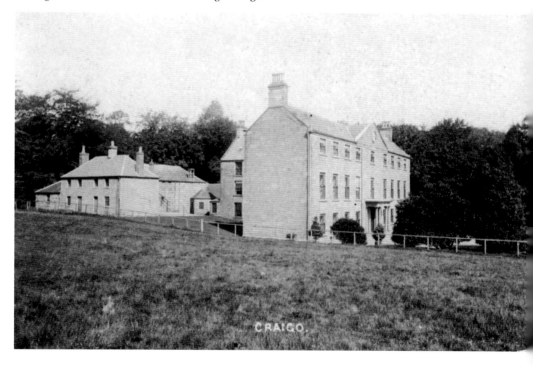

CRAIGO.

MULTIVIEW & NOVELTY POSTCARDS

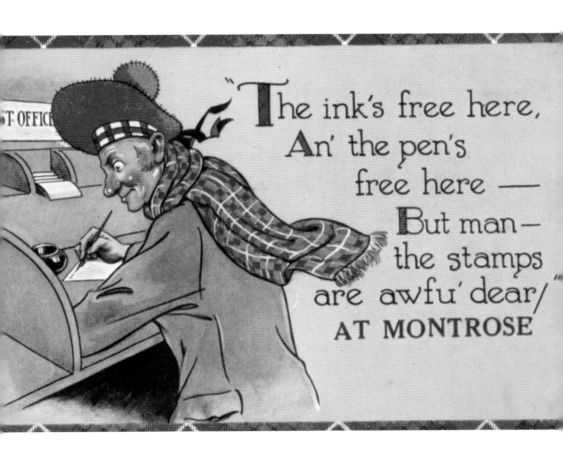

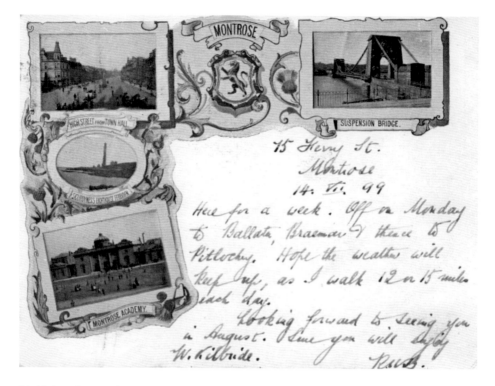

Multiview Postcards

The postcard above is an early court size, dated 1899, of the High Street, Suspension Bridge, Scurdyness Lighthouse and the Academy. The *c.* 1940 postcard below shows Scurdyness Lighthouse, the New Bridge, Panmure Gardens and Academy, and the High Street from the north and south.

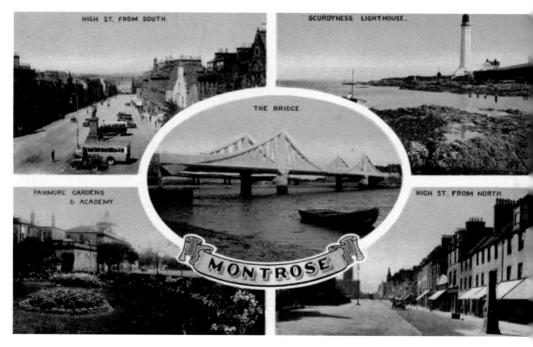

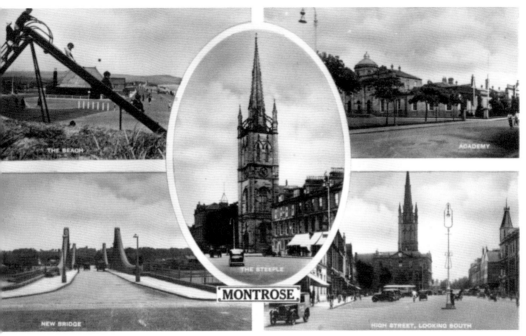

Multiview Postcards

The late 1930s postcard above shows the beach, the Academy, the New Bridge, the Steeple and the High Street looking south. The 'Everything going well at Montrose' postcard on the right shows the High Street, New Bridge, and Scurdyness Lighthouse, and is dated 1937.

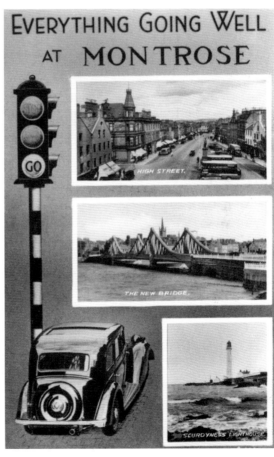

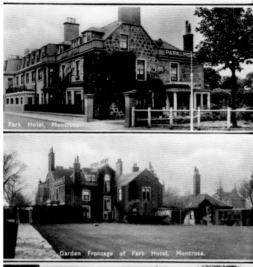

Greetings from Montrose

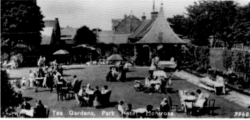

Multiview Postcards

The 'Greetings from Montrose' postcard on the left shows three different views of the Park Hotel in John Street around 1937. The postcard below shows a general view of Montrose, Scurdyness Lighthouse, and the Suspension Bridge, and is dated 1908.

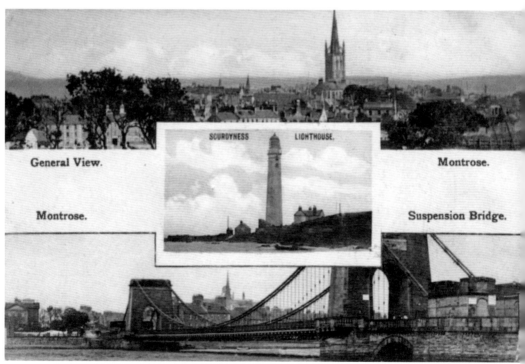

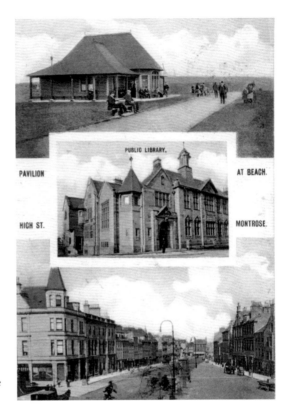

Multiview Postcards
The top postcard shows the Beach Pavilion, the public library and the High Street, and is dated 1908. The bottom postcard shows the West End Park, North Esk Road and the bowling green around 1908.

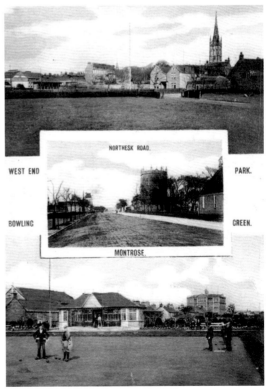

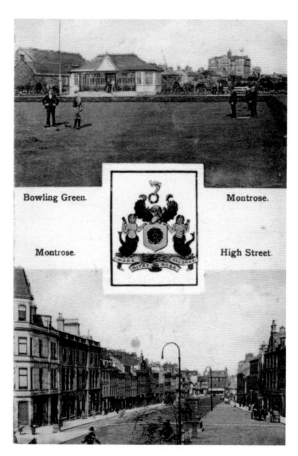

Bowling Green.

Montrose.

Montrose.

High Street.

Multiview Postcards

The postcard on the left shows the bowling green and the High Street, with the Montrose coat of arms in the centre. The postcard below shows Ferryden and Red Castle at Lunan Bay, with the Montrose coat of arms at the top, and is dated 1912.

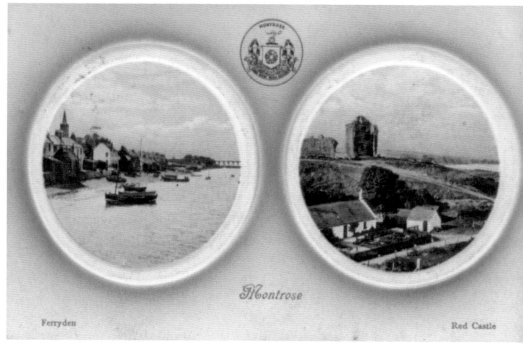

Montrose

Ferryden

Red Castle

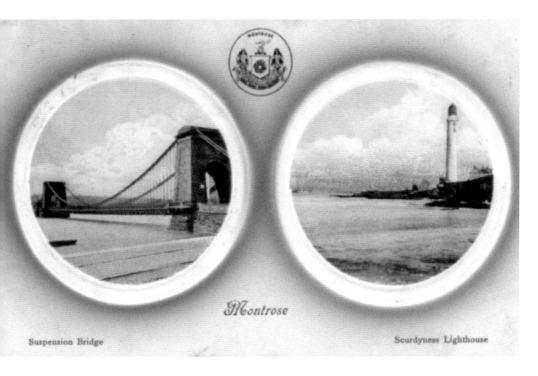

Montrose

Suspension Bridge   Scurdyness Lighthouse

Multiview Postcards

The postcard above shows the Suspension Bridge and Scurdyness Lighthouse, with the Montrose coat of arms at the top, and is dated 1909. The postcard below shows Rossie Castle and Rossie Gardens, again with the Montrose coat of arms at the top, and is dated 1909.

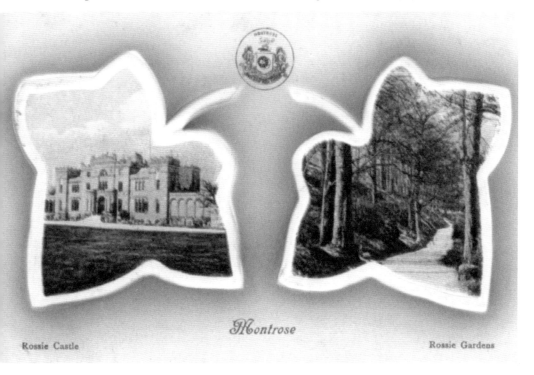

Montrose

Rossie Castle   Rossie Gardens

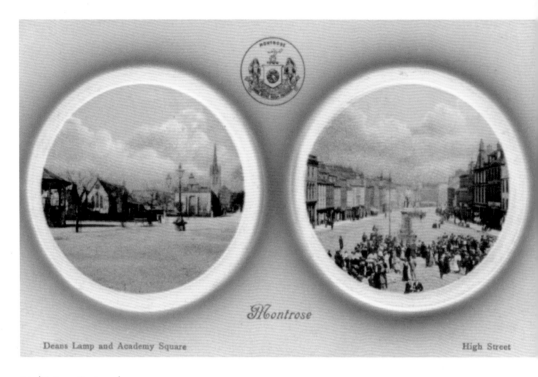

Deans Lamp and Academy Square   High Street

Multiview Postcards

The postcard above shows the Dean Lamp and Academy Square on the left, and the High Street on the right, with the Montrose coat of arms at the top around 1908. Below we see Scurdyness Lighthouse and Peel Place with the Montrose coat of arms on the left, and is dated 1907.

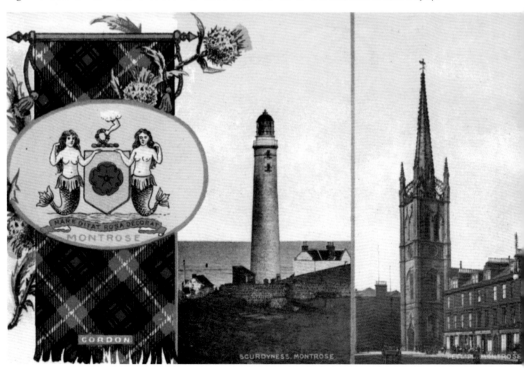

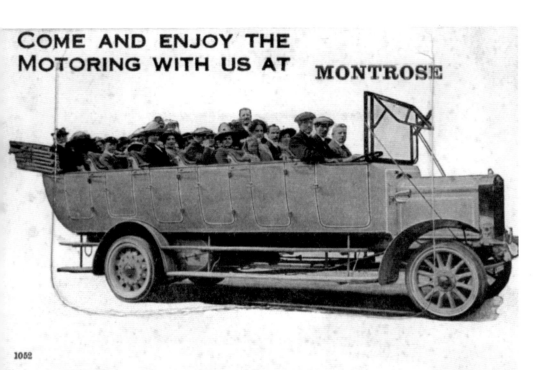

Novelty Postcards
'Come and Enjoy the Motoring with us at Montrose', dated 1920, and 'Having a High Old Time at Montrose', dated 1913. These novelty pull-out postcards contain twelve miniature postcard views.

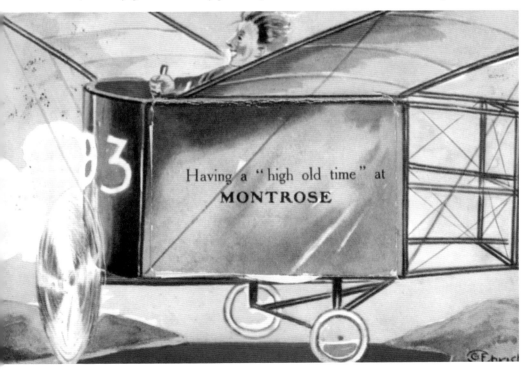

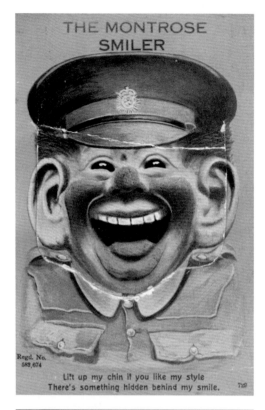

THE MONTROSE
SMILER

Regd. No.
589,674

Lift up my chin if you like my style
There's something hidden behind my smile.

720

Novelty Postcards
More pull-out postcards: 'The Montrose
Smiler', dated 1912, and 'Just Arrived First-class,
at Montrose', dated 1915.

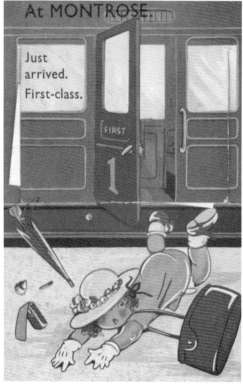

At MONTROSE

Just
arrived.
First-class.

FIRST

1

SECTION 11
AERIAL VIEWS

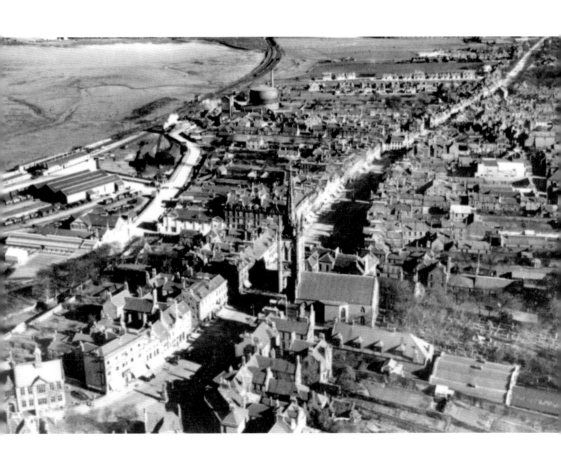

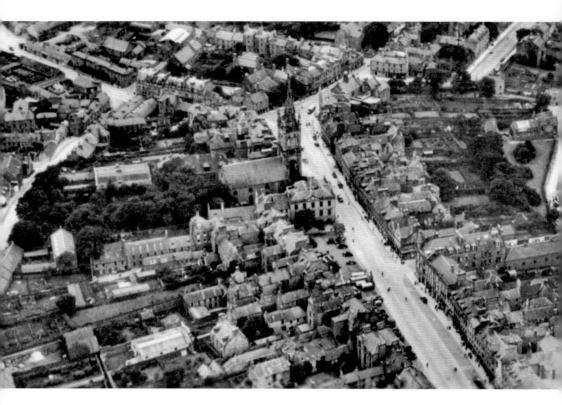

Aerial Views

As the aeroplane became more widely used between 1920 and 1940, postcard publishers were soon having photographs of town and cities taken from the air. The view above is looking south down the High Street, while the view below is looking north up Peel Place and the High Street; both show the old church steeple.

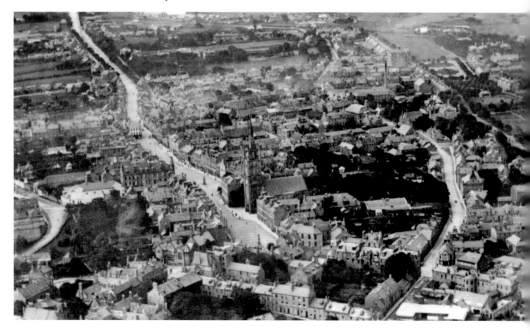

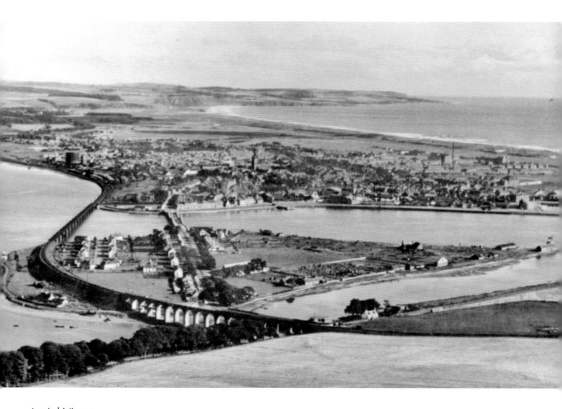

Aerial Views

The view above is looking north and shows Rossie Island, the railway bridge and the new bridge. The view below is again looking north, showing the two bridges and Bridge Street.

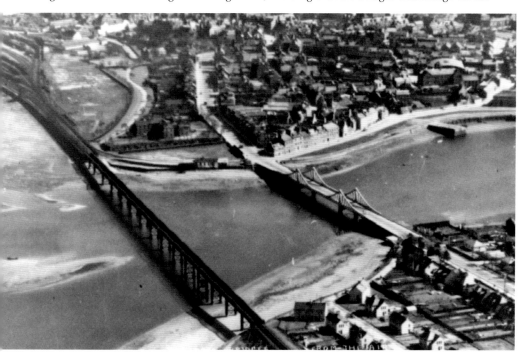

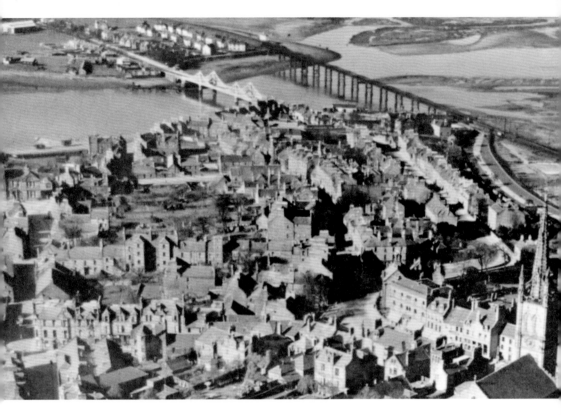

Aerial Views
The view above is looking south down Bridge Street to the two bridges. The view below shows the north end of the Mid Links. The North Links School can be seen to the right and Dorward House near the bottom.

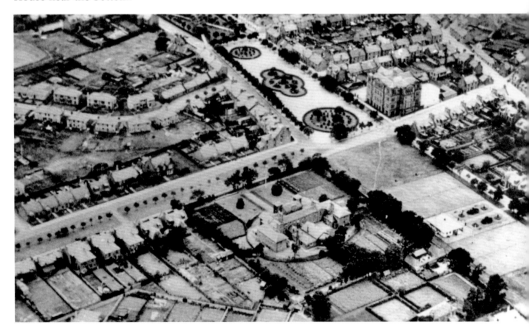